READING IN THE CONTENT AREAS
SCIENCE 1

Laura Stark Johnson

PERMISSIONS

AMERICAN CHEMICAL SOCIETY for "Grandma, the Airport, and RoboCop" by Eric J. Blendermann.

AMERICAN WATER WORKS ASSOCIATION for "Water Trivia Facts."

MARGARET COOPER for "Gift from the Sun" from *Gift from the Sun: The Mastering of Energy* by Margaret Cooper, Bradbury Press, Englewood Cliffs, New Jersey, © 1969.

FACTS ON FILE, INC., for "Thermometers." From *How Everyday Things Work* by Chris Cooper and Tony Osman. Copyright © 1984 by Orbis Publishing Ltd. Reprinted with permission of Facts On File, Inc., New York.

FRANKLIN WATTS, INC. for "Your Immune Defense System." From *Your Immune System,* Copyright © 1989 by Alan E. Nourse. Reprinted with permission of the publisher, Franklin Watts, Inc.

GROLIER, INC., for "Water." Reprinted with permission of *The New Book of Knowledge,* copyright 1990, Grolier, Inc.

HARCOURT BRACE JOVANOVICH, INC., for "Spare Parts for People." Excerpts from *Spare Parts for People,* copyright © 1987 by Margery Facklam and Howard Facklam, reprinted by permission of Harcourt Brace Jovanovich, Inc.

HOLT, RINEHART AND WINSTON, INC., for "Bees." Excerpt from "Bees" from *Exploring and Understanding Insects* by Barbara J. Collins, copyright © 1970 by Holt, Rinehart and Winston, Inc., reprinted by permission of the publisher.

for "What Is Vinegar?" from *Exploring and Understanding Chemistry* by Charles D. Neal, James N. Cummins, and Charles R. Heinz, copyright © 1970 by Holt, Rinehart and Winston, Inc., reprinted by permission of the publisher.

GEORGE LILES for "Science Looks Twice at Twins."

MACMILLAN PUBLISHING COMPANY for "Skin." Reprinted with permission of Macmillan Publishing Company from *Macmillan Book of the Human Body* by Mary Elting. Text, Copyright © 1986 by Mary Elting.

for "Eureka! I Found It!" Reprinted with permission of Atheneum Publishers, an imprint of Macmillan Publishing Company from *Secrets of the Universe* by Paul Fleisher. Illustrated by Patricia Keeler. Text copyright © 1987 Paul Fleisher. Illustrations copyright © 1987 Patricia A. Keeler.

NATIONAL GEOGRAPHIC SOCIETY for "Egg Float" and "At the Water's Edge." Reprinted by permission, National Geographic Books for World Explorers. Copyright © 1986 National Geographic Society.

THE ORLANDO SENTINEL for "How They Crumble" by Charlotte Balcomb Lane, May 3, 1990.

PUBLICOM, INC., for the writing of "Science, a Multihuman Activity" by Betty B. Hoskins, Ph.D., and for the writing of "What Makes Climates Change?" by Maurice J. Sabean.

RANDOM HOUSE, INC., for "Smaller than Molecules." From *The Story of the Atom* by Mae and Ira Freeman. Copyright © 1960 by Mae Freeman and Ira Freeman. Text copyright renewed 1988 by John B. Freeman. Illustrations copyright renewed 1988 by Random House, Inc. Reprinted by permission of Random House, Inc.

SIMON AND SCHUSTER, INC. for "Shopping Cart" and "Traffic Light." From the book *Why Didn't I Think of That?* By Webb Garrison, illustrated by Ray Abel © 1977. Used by permission of the publisher, Prentice Hall/A division of Simon & Schuster, Inc., Englewood Cliffs, N.J. 07632.

UNIVERSITY OF ALASKA for "Blue Babe—a Messenger from the Ice Age" by Gary Selinger, *University of Alaska Magazine,* June 1986.

WAYLAND (PUBLISHERS) LIMITED for "The Earth We Live On" and "Moving Continents." From *Mountains and Earth Movements* by Iain Bain. Reprinted by permission of Wayland (Publishers) Limited, 61 Western Road, Hove, East Sussex BN3 1JD, England.

WESTERN PUBLISHING COMPANY, INC., for "What Physics Is, and How We Use It." From *The Wonders of Physics* by Irving Adler © 1966 Western Publishing Company, Inc. Used by Permission.

WESTMINSTER/JOHN KNOX PRESS for "Frozen Foods," altered from *How Do They Make It?,* by George Sullivan. Copyright © MCMLXV George Sullivan. Altered and used by permission of Westminster/John Knox Press.

WILLIAM MORROW AND COMPANY, INC., for "Space Junk" from *Space Junk* by Judy Donnelly and Sydelle Kramer. Text: Copyright © 1990. By permission of Morrow Junior Books, a division of William Morrow and Co., Inc.

ISBN 0-88336-121-3

Copyright © 1991
New Readers Press
Publishing Division of Laubach Literacy International
1320 Jamesville Ave., Syracuse, New York 13210

Sponsoring Editor: Christina M. Jagger
Project Editor: Heidi Stephens
Cover Design: Patricia Rapple
Cover Art: Stephen Rhodes

9 8 7 6

Table of Contents

What do you think of when you hear the words "scientific research"? Do you picture a lone scientist peering through a microscope in a laboratory? As the title of this selection suggests, science is really an effort by many people working together. Read to learn about what science is and how science is done.

Science,
a Multihuman Activity

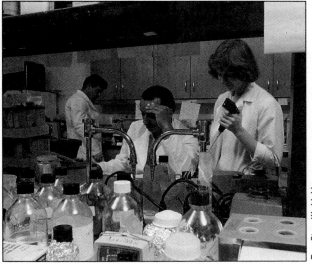

Tony Stone Worldwide

Science is a major part of our daily lives. This "recipe" shows how it works:

1. Start with a good question.
2. Think of several possible answers.
3. Add ideas on how to test for the true answers.
4. Work with a team to investigate the ideas.
5. Find ways to apply the answers usefully.

In applying the answers usefully, science leads us to its partner—technology.[1] Technology is more visible to the public than pure science is. The tools of technology apply scientific findings to product development.

Science has been an activity of human beings for thousands of years. It started with hunters and gatherers, who had to figure out the seasons to hunt for animals and to search for edible roots, berries, and nuts. Our ancestors were curious about the regular return of the seasons. They built Stonehenge and Mayan pyramids to mark the longest and shortest days, and to observe the two dates each year with equal days and nights (the equinoxes). As people watched the regularly changing patterns of stars in the sky, they told stories of the constellations, and they constructed the first calendars.

Today, however, curiosity and charts are just the start of a scientific investigation. The true answer to a

---

1. technology: applied science; the use of scientific knowledge to provide objects or tools for human use

question may not even fit with ordinary observations and common sense! Between prehistory and now, in building the current theories[2] many people have worked together to collect facts and to see if observations and experiments can be repeated. If they can be repeated, then they are probably valid.[3]

Through the ages, people's work has been and continues to be influenced by the society around them. Society's ideas about the nature of human beings, about the chemical and physical laws of the environment, and about cities and nations all have an effect on what people study, what results they obtain, and what interpretations they make. This means that new information can modify[4] scientific theory.

The "way that science is done" evolves, too. Now the activities of science, including technology, are carried out by groups of people. The principal scientist turns to less senior scientists and the laboratory technicians who carry out the experiments. The engineer talks over the computer program with the design team and perhaps with a spouse. The department secretary transforms a rough draft of the investigator's grant proposal into the form required by the officials at the government agency. Behind the scenes, many people are maintaining the heating, ventilation, and air-conditioning, as well as the cleanliness of the labs and the rest of the building.

The setting might be a university, an industrial complex, a medical center, or an independent research laboratory.

Many of the scientists were trained in laboratories in the same country as the university or other setting, but foreign students and investigators come to their lab to work. Some have immigrated or are refugees; some study a while and then share their training upon returning to their countries of birth.

Science is an open, multinational undertaking. Scientists travel to meetings where they look at each other's data and argue each other's interpretations. Before releasing news to the popular media, such as television or newspapers, they publish the results of their experiments in scientific journals. In order to be published, the articles must first be reviewed by the scientists' peers.[5]

For centuries, any interested persons could know most of the scientific discoveries of their age. They could keep track of what was new in physics, or chemistry, or biology, or earth science. Now, the rate of new information is so great that we have to be content[6] with an overview. There is time to delve into only those areas that interest us most. As you read the articles in this book, notice that the fields of science are all interrelated. Then be prepared for the newspapers, magazines, radio, and television to continue adding to your overview of science—there is always something new.

---

2. **theories:** ideas offered to explain something
3. **valid:** true in all situations
4. **modify:** change
5. **peers:** equals; fellow members of a group, in this case the community of scientists
6. **content:** satisfied

Written by Publicom, Inc./Betty B. Hoskins, Ph.D.

Unit 1: Biology

the science that deals with the study of living things

THE PEACEABLE KINGDOM, Edward Hicks, 1780-1849; Worcester Art Museum, Worcester, Massachusetts

Have you ever set off the metal detector at an airport? Did you find out what was on you that triggered the alarm? Read about Grandma's experience with a metal detector, and discover what she and the movie character RoboCop have in common.

Grandma, the Airport, and RoboCop

There was one thing about airports that always scared Ricky a little bit: the metal detectors you had to walk through to get to your plane. They always made him uneasy, because he never was sure whether he'd set them off or not; he never quite knew what *would* set them off. He had asked Oma, his grandmother, why there had to be metal detectors in airports at all. "Hijackers," was her brisk reply, which didn't help much, because Ricky didn't know what a hijacker was, either.

Ricky's curiosity got the better of him. "Oma," he asked as they waited in line to go through the metal detector for the flight home from San Diego, "what is a hijacker, anyway?"

"A hijacker, my young friend," said Oma, "is an evil person who steals a plane or a truck or a car and makes it go somewhere other than where it's supposed to go. A hijacker is a criminal. Now, hush up about hijackers!"

Oma took Ricky's hand when it was their turn to walk through the metal detector, and they were almost through the scanner when beeeeeeeep! they set off the alarm!

"Excuse me, ma'am," said the airport security guard. "Would you please step back through the machine and try it again? You and the little guy go through one at a time, please."

Ricky was terrified. What if he had set off the alarm?!? He tried to think:

GATES 1-17

What do I have in my pockets? Could he get in trouble for taking Twizzlers[1] on an airplane?

Oma led Ricky back through the metal detector, then said, "Go ahead, Rick. You go through, then I'll go through."

Ricky closed his eyes tight, then stepped through the scanner—and didn't set it off! He was okay! He wasn't a hijacker! He wasn't going to jail!

Then Oma stepped into the scanner and beeeeeeep! set off the alarm again! The guard said, "Would you empty your pockets, please, ma'am?" as another guard hurried over from the other line. Horrified, Ricky thought, Is

Oma a hijacker? Why would she steal a plane? Where would she put it?

"I'm afraid I haven't any pockets, sir," Oma said, "but I do have this to show you," and she fished out of her purse a card that was laminated in plastic. The security guard looked at the card and said "Aha!" then showed the card to the other guard, who nodded her head.

"Okay, ma'am, you can board the plane," said the guard. "Sorry for the hassle; you do understand that we need to be careful, I hope."

"Of course, sir," Oma replied. "I understand completely; you were only

---

1. Twizzlers: brand name of a licorice candy

Grandma, the Airport, and RoboCop   9

doing your job to keep the airline safe. Thank you very much."

"Thank you, ma'am," the guard called after them as Oma hustled Ricky down the ramp toward the gate, where the flight attendants were already boarding passengers on the flight home. Ricky's head was buzzing with questions, but Oma shushed him each time he started to ask, so in the end he took his seat on the plane in puzzled silence.

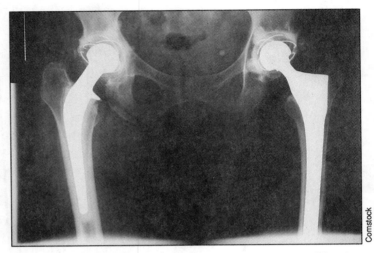

An X-ray shows hip implants. Notice how far the replacement parts extend down into the bones of the legs.

The plane took off smoothly, and Ricky watched the ground drop away and away and away, until they were in the clouds and then above the clouds, where the sunshine was very bright. Oma was chatting and laughing with a woman across the aisle, while Ricky stared out the window at the fantastic, dazzling white mountains and valleys in the clouds. Before long, the flight attendants served lunch that was called "Poulet Fricassee Alouette," which apparently meant chicken with a lot of pepper on it. Ricky dug in hungrily.

"Well, Ricky," Oma asked after a while, "would you like to know what happened back there at the metal detector in the airport? Or are you more interested in putting that entire chicken in your mouth in one bite?"

"No, tell me," Ricky managed to say around a mouthful of chicken. "How come you set off the detector? You don't

have anything metal on your dress or your arms or anything."

"Actually, I have some metal inside me," Oma said. "That's what set off the alarm."

Ricky stared, wide-eyed, while Oma went on. "Do you remember last year, when I fell down and broke my hip? I was in the hospital for a long time, remember? You sent me all those get-well cards."

"I remember that," said Ricky. "How come you went to the hospital? Mom said you just fell down on the sidewalk." Ricky himself fell down on the sidewalk with some regularity.

"That's right, I fell on the sidewalk. But it's different for an old woman like me to fall down than it is for a strong young man like yourself. My bones are old, Ricky, and they don't heal like yours would if you fell down and broke your hip. In my case, my doctor decided to replace my broken hip with a new one, one that's made out of metal and ceramics."

"Huh? Ceramics?" Ricky's mind was already reeling, and this was yet another new word for him.

"Ceramics are like the china that my teacups are made out of, or the tiles in your bathroom. Those materials are called ceramics, Ricky, and part of my new hip is made out of those materials. But it was the metal in my hip that set off the metal detector; my doctor warned me about that, and he gave me a card to show the guards in case it happened."

"You've got a metal hip!" Ricky exclaimed. What a thought! "Like a robot!" Robo-Oma!

"Heavens, no! I'm not a robot, you silly thing. I've just got a few artificial parts in me; they do it all the time nowadays, my doctor said, and Ricky, I want to tell you, this new hip makes it easier for me to walk than it has been for years!"

At this point, the woman across the aisle leaned over and said, "Your grandmother's right, young fellow; people are getting new parts pretty often these days. It wasn't possible, not too long ago; we didn't have materials that the body would accept. Now, though, there are scientists making new alloys and ceramics that work just fine in artificial joints, like your grandmother's hip."

"What's an alloy?" Ricky asked. "And who are you?"

"Ricky, don't you be rude," scolded Oma. "This is Dr. Merrell. She's a chemist, and she works on making the plastics that go into artificial hearts. She may even have worked on the materials that are in my hip."

"Well, no," laughed Dr. Merrell, "it's unlikely that any of my work is in your hip; I'm into plastics. I have enough trouble making things that people's bodies will accept, without trying to learn metals and ceramics, too!"

Dr. Merrell looked at Ricky. "To answer your question, an alloy is a blend of different metals that has some characteristics that the metals don't have when they're alone. Chemists can concoct different alloys to do different jobs. It's the same with ceramics and plastics; the first thing you have to do when you're making a material to use inside someone's body is figure out what you want that material to do.

"You might want your material—I'll call it 'stuff'—to be solid and smooth, so parts of the body won't stick to it. The joint in your grandmother's hip is like that. If tissue starts growing into the joint itself, it'll hurt her a lot when she moves. But maybe you want to make some kind of artificial bone stuff, for someone who has lost some bone tissue. Then you want to make stuff that the rest of the bone will grow into, grab onto, so that eventually it'll seem like it's all natural bone.

"Have you ever had a filling put in your teeth, Ricky?" Ricky's answer was a slow nod, as he remembered his first cavity with shame. "Well, that stuff that the dentist put into your tooth to fill up your cavity, that was a material that had to start out soft, so it would fill the hole in your tooth, then had to get very hard, so it could stand all your chewing." Dr.

Merrell smiled. "And, that stuff had to be waterproof, because your mouth is a very wet place!"

"What about robots?" Ricky blurted out. "I saw *RoboCop*. How did they put all that metal into that guy's head? And he had metal arms and legs!"

"Ricky, that was just a movie!" laughed Oma, but Dr. Merrell smiled at Ricky and nodded her head.

"That's right, Ricky, they did put a lot of metal into that guy, didn't they? Well, your grandmother's right; that was a movie, and we can't put a body back together like they did in *RoboCop*, but there are people who have lost arms and legs who now have artificial limbs that work nearly as well as their natural ones. We try very hard to make artificial skin that feels natural and matches the person's natural color; a lot of artificial skin is used to help heal people who've been badly burned. There are doctors and scientists who have built artificial hearts for people whose hearts have stopped working; other scientists have developed tiny, flexible tubes to substitute for veins or arteries that have collapsed or deteriorated.

"We can't build whole new bodies for people yet, Ricky, but, with the new materials that we can use, stuff that's designed for whatever job we want to do, we can rebuild a lot of parts of people who've been injured, to help them recover from their injuries and get on with their lives."

"Like I did, Ricky," added Oma. "I'd rather have natural joints that worked, of course, but if it's a choice for me between my old, broken-down hip and this metal one that lets me walk so easily, I'll take the metal one every time. Even if it *does* set off the metal detector."

"I don't mind that, Oma," Ricky said as he reached for his pudding. "It's pretty cool having a grandmother who's part robot."

Dr. Merrell laughed at that; Oma harrumphed and picked up her magazine, shaking her head, but inside she was smiling.

"Grandma, the Airport, and RoboCop," by Eric J. Blendermann, from an American Chemical Society newspaper supplement

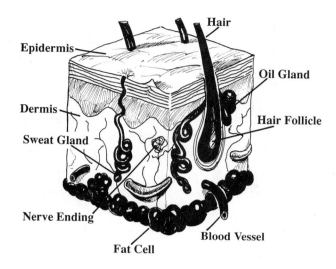

Epidermis — Hair — Oil Gland — Dermis — Hair Follicle — Sweat Gland — Nerve Ending — Blood Vessel — Fat Cell

Skin

Did you know that people shed their skin? Before you begin this selection, think about what you know about the skin. Then read to learn some interesting facts that may surprise you.

As you grow, your skin has to cover more and more territory. Does it just keep stretching? For a long time people thought so. But at last scientists figured out what the skin is really like.

Your skin is made of three main layers. The inside layer, called the *dermis,* is the thickest. Next comes a layer of soft, plump, almost square cells.[1] On top of that middle layer is a sheet of thin material something like kitchen plastic wrap. The middle and top layers are called the *epidermis*. This is where some fascinating things go on.

For a while the cells in the middle layer do nothing unusual. Then each cell grows slightly bigger and divides into two smaller cells. These

---

1. cells: basic units of living matter, of which all plants and animals are made

grow to full size, and then they divide, making four cells. These divide into eight, then 16, and so on.

As the cells multiply, some of them are pushed outward. Their shape changes. They grow flatter and begin to die. Finally, the dead cells overlap each other and cling together tightly in a tough, almost waterproof film. This is the top layer of the epidermis that covers the whole outside of your body.

It takes almost two months for a cell to be pushed all the way to the surface. Cells beneath it keep moving up, forcing it and many others all the way out—until at last little bunches of dead cells curl up into loose flakes. So many skin flakes leave your body every day that they can actually be seen when a shaft of light comes into a room. The specks that we call dust floating in the air are mostly flakes of skin cells! Every hour you shed about one million dead skin cells. At the end of a month, you will have an almost completely new epidermis.

The new cells don't form at a steady rate. Around midnight, one of your body clocks gives a signal for increased production. From then until about 4 o'clock in the morning, skin cells divide more quickly than at any other time of day. So, if you take a bath in the morning, the ring in your tub consists of more dead skin cells than it does if you take a bath at night.

Skin cells also form the lining of your nose, mouth, and throat and continue down through your lungs, stomach, and intestines. The skin cells in your tongue multiply very fast at night. Look at your tongue in the mirror just before you go to bed. It will be mostly pink with some white down the middle. In the morning, before brushing your teeth, look again. You will see more of a white coat than the night before. With your fingernail gently scrape the top of your tongue, and a bit of thick white stuff called mucus will come off. In it are thousands of dead skin cells that were shed during the night.

Your Skin at Work

One scientist calls the skin a "miracle wrap" because it does so many wonderful things.

By making new cells all the time, your skin can mend itself every time you get a scrape or cut. Special cells in your skin protect you against sunburn. When a lot of sunlight hits them, these cells produce a brownish substance called *melanin*. Gradually the melanin creeps into other cells and gives them a darker color. The dark cells keep harmful rays of sunlight from burning the sensitive cells underneath.

Your "miracle wrap" helps keep your whole body from getting too hot. Millions of little air conditioners called *sweat glands* are built into the dermis. These coils of cells produce sweat—a mixture of water and chemicals. When sweat reaches the top layer of skin, it evaporates and carries away heat. An adult's sweat glands produce about two or three cups of water on an ordinary warm day. But in very hot weather the glands really go into action. Exercise makes them work harder, too. During exercise, they can produce as much as 10 cups of sweat an hour, provided the person drinks enough water!

Where does all that water come from? The glands draw some of it out of tiny blood vessels nearby in the dermis. The rest comes from lymph, a liquid that constantly bathes the body's cells.

Your skin gives you information about what is going on in the outside world. The clear covering at the front of each eye—the cornea—is a special kind of skin that lets in light, so you can see.

Scattered all through the dermis are the tips of nerves that send messages to the brain. Some of the messages tell you that you are cold, or

An adult who may produce three cups of sweat on an ordinary warm day can produce as much as 10 cups during exercise.

warn you to stand back from a hot stove. Others tell you when something hurts. And still other messages let you know about somebody's soft, comforting touch when you feel sad.

Your skin keeps your delicate inside parts from drying out. It also keeps germs from getting in. And there are plenty of germs ready and waiting to get in. You have more bacteria and other tiny living things called yeasts on your skin than there are people on earth! They are so tiny that a dozen or more of them could roost on the point of a pin. Their food is the dead cells that come off in flakes from the outside layer of skin. Germs multiply very, very fast. But most of them live only about 80 minutes.

Luckily, most of the germs that live on your skin don't cause you any problems. They don't make you sick. But just in case a harmful one shows up, your skin has a thin film of chemicals that control some germs. Some people even have certain bacteria on their skin that produce a substance called an *antibiotic*. It actually kills harmful bacteria and keeps cuts from getting infected.

No wonder skin is called a "miracle wrap."

From the *Macmillan Book of the Human Body,* by Mary Elting

Do you know any twins? How are they alike? How are they different? By studying twins, especially identical twins, scientists learn a lot about how we come to be the people we are. Read to see what we can learn from the study of twins.

Science Looks

Twice at Twins

If twins interest you, Twinsburg will fascinate you.

Every summer since 1976, this little town outside Cleveland, Ohio, has been invaded by twins. Last summer 2,356 sets of twins showed up from around the world to watch and take part in parades, fireworks, magic acts, a five kilometer race, and more than 100 contests: contests to honor the oldest twins, the youngest, the most alike, the least alike, the twins with the widest combined smile.

Had you been there, you might have noticed a small army of "infiltrators"[1]—scientists who also attend the festival. Some come seeking clues to the causes of health problems—skin diseases, cancer, and multiple sclerosis, for example. Others are interested in how it feels to be a twin. But of all the scientists, perhaps the ones doing the most important—and most controversial—work are those who study *nature and nurture,* that age-old question of how we come to be the kind of people we are.

Why are some of us good at math, or writing, while others excel at art or basketball? What causes the differences in our intelligence, talents, and tastes? Are they largely set by the genes[2] we inherit from our parents (nature)? How much do our experiences in life (nurture)—the *environment* we grow up in—have to do with it?

If you were a scientist interested in this question, wouldn't you love to study identical twins? Just think of it: two people who developed from the same fertilized egg, or *zygote.* That is, two people with the exact same set of genes. Any differences between such *monozygotic* (from one zygote) twins would have to be the result of differences in their environment. But could you also say that any similarities were the result of having the same genes?

Not really. Remember, most twins share a similar environment—same house, food, relatives, and so on. The only way you could accurately measure the effects of nature and nurture would

---

1. **infiltrators:** people who slip through or pass into a place, often to spy
2. **genes:** tiny parts of cells that are passed from parents to children and that determine or affect the children's characteristics, such as height and hair color

be to study identical twins *raised apart,* in different environments.

Over the last 10 years, a team of scientists led by psychologist[3] Thomas J. Bouchard, Jr., has studied about 65 pairs of identical twins who were raised apart (called *MZAs,* for "monozygotic apart"). (They've also studied about 45 fraternal[4] twins who were raised apart—called *DZAs,* for "dizygotic[5] apart.")

The scientists bring each pair of twins to the University of Minnesota for a week of intensive testing. Doctors and dentists on the team give the twins thorough physical examinations. They record the twins' height, weight, eye color, ear shape, and head length.

Meanwhile, psychologists give the twins IQ[6] and personality tests. To measure personality, the psychologists try to determine things like how much the twins worry, whether they are cautious or reckless, and how creative they are. They measure these and other traits by the twins' responses to statements such as: "I rarely, if ever, do anything reckless," and "The crackle and flames of a wood fire stimulate my imagination." By the week's end, each twin has answered about 15,000 questions.

Bouchard's team believes they have found some startling similarities in the twins raised apart. They say the twins often have surprisingly similar gestures and postures, for instance. In pictures, many of the twins strike nearly identical poses. And some of the MZAs discover they have led remarkably similar lives.

The first set of MZA twins Bouchard studied, the "Jim twins," were adopted by different families four weeks after they were born. They grew up in Ohio, 45 miles away from each other. When they were reunited at the age of 39, they discovered a series of quirky similarities. Both were named Jim. Both drove the same model blue Chevrolet, liked woodworking, chewed their fingernails, and owned dogs named Toy. Both started having late-afternoon headaches at the age of 18.

The sort of similarities the Jim twins discovered are common with the twins the Minnesota team has studied. Some critics of the Minnesota study say the coincidences are not surprising. They argue that everyone's life has enough details that a number of coincidences are bound to exist. What's more, for every coincidence a pair of MZAs discovers, a skeptic could point to a vast number of undiscovered *differences.* The same two twins might have different model television sets and root for different football teams. But the differences would go unreported since they would not surprise anyone.

But beyond the coincidences, the Minnesota scientists have gathered and analyzed a mountain of data about the twins' health, intelligence, and personalities. And according to Bouchard, the MZA data show clearly that nature—the genes we inherit— exerts a notably strong influence over our lives. The Minnesota team has found

---

3. **psychologist:** scientist who studies the actions, thoughts, and feelings of people
4. **fraternal:** of the same or opposite sex and coming from two separately fertilized egg cells
5. **dizygotic:** from two separate zygotes, or fertilized eggs
6. **IQ:** abbreviation for Intelligence Quotient; a number used to express a person's intelligence

Pictured above are four of the five sets of twins who attended the same elementary school in Brandenburg, Kentucky, in 1987. Try to tell which pairs are identical twins and which are fraternal twins.

that MZAs are remarkably similar in physical traits such as height, fingerprints, and heart rates. Adult MZAs also tend to have similar medical histories, developing the eye disease glaucoma at the same time, for example.

The Minnesota team has reported that intelligence also seems to be influenced much more by genes than by environment. Despite being raised by different families, separated identical twins studied by Bouchard's team earned identical or nearly identical scores on adult intelligence tests.

But most surprisingly, the Minnesota team claims that their study shows clearly that genes play a big part in shaping our personalities—helping to determine whether we respect tradition and like to follow rules, for example, or whether we're dedicated nonconformists.[7] According to Bouchard, the genes you were born with have a lot to do with whether you are confident, cheerful, and upbeat, or whether you feel, say, that the world is out to get you. "The study shows in a very persuasive way that genes influence every aspect of behavior," says Nancy Segal, a psychologist with the Minnesota team.

Other scientists disagree. How can you study whether intelligence is inherited, they ask, when there are so many different ways just to define intelligence? The problem applies to other traits, they say.

---

7. **nonconformists:** people who do not follow customs or practices that are usual for a given place or time

Twins: Born of Chance and Yams?

Two identical twins marry two other identical twins. What are the chances that the couples will have identical twins themselves?

About 1 in 270—no better or worse than the odds for anyone else, says Thomas J. Bouchard, Jr., psychologist at the University of Minnesota in Minneapolis. That's because the chances of having identical twins are not influenced by genetics.

Genetics does, however, play a role in the production of fraternal twins, which requires two eggs from the mother. Certain genes may cause a woman to release more than one egg during her monthly cycle of ovulation,[8] says Bouchard. That may be why fraternal twins tend to run in the family.

Genetics could also be the reason that certain ethnic groups tend to have more fraternal twins than others, says Bouchard—why African-American women, for example, tend to have more fraternal twins than whites, who have more than either Japanese, Chinese, or Native Americans.

Older women and women who already have had kids tend to have more fraternal twins, says Bouchard. With age and many births, a woman's body becomes "less precise" at releasing only one egg during ovulation, he says.

Diet is another possible factor. Incredibly, yams may be a major reason the Yoruba tribe of Nigeria has one of the highest fraternal twinning rates in the world. Yorubas love the mushy orange vegetables and eat them almost every day. Yams, according to the hypothesis,[9] contain a substance much like the female hormone[10] that triggers the release of two eggs.

Similarly, fertility drugs[11] can sometimes make an infertile woman release several eggs. Once childless, she can end up with several babies all at once.

The twins studies have not ended the nature/nurture debate, especially on the questions of intelligence and personality. And Bouchard himself points out that even the most closely matched twins on record are different from each other. So even though genes have a strong influence over our lives, they are not the only influence. Our day-to-day experiences help to mold us, too.

8. **ovulation:** process in which an unfertilized egg is released by one of a woman's two ovaries, the female reproductive organs
9. **hypothesis:** a possible way to explain an event based on what is already known or observed
10. **hormone:** a substance produced in one part of the body that travels by the bloodstream to another part of the body and affects the activity of cells there
11. **fertility drugs:** medicines prescribed by doctors to increase the chances that an egg will be fertilized

"Science Looks Twice at Twins," by George Liles, previously published in *Science World*

Have you ever heard of the Universal Donor Card? Many people carry one in their wallets, but even they may not know about all it can mean. Read this selection to find out about organ donation—a way to provide "spare parts for people."

LifeLink of Florida

Organ Donor Card

John Doe

Print or type name of donor

In the hope that I may help others, I hereby make this anatomical gift, if medically acceptable, to take effect upon my death. The words and marks below indicate my desires.

I give:
(a) _____ any needed organs or tissue
(b) _____ only the following organs or tissue

Specify the organ(s) or tissue _____

for the purposes of transplantation, therapy, medical research or education;
(c) _____ my body for anatomical study if needed.

Limitations or special wishes, if any: _____

Patty DiRienzo

Spare Parts

.... *for People*

How do you ask a man for his son's heart?

Where do you find a healthy liver that could save a child's life?

It's not easy. Not a day goes by without the chance for one person's tragedy to turn into another person's miracle.

John was an 18-year-old high school senior riding home from football practice one August night when a car sideswiped his motorcycle, leaving him "brain-dead." His EEG (electroencephalogram[1])

recorded no brain waves, nor was there a single response to any of the other standard and absolutely decisive tests for life, even while John's heart and lungs were kept working on a respirator.

Several months before the accident, John and his family had watched a television program about transplants, and they had talked about organ donation. In the midst of their shock and grief over their son's death, John's

---

1. **electroencephalogram:** lines drawn by a machine as it records brain activity

parents didn't want to think about anyone else's problems. But they remembered that John had thought organ donation was a great idea, and they gave the hospital permission to use his healthy organs. Within hours, John's heart was on its way to a 39-year-old father of four. One kidney was given to a young science teacher, and the other was transplanted into a 17-year-old waitress who had been surviving on kidney dialysis[2] for four years. John's liver was transplanted into a 19-year-old college student, and two other people were able to see again with the corneas from John's eyes.

Each year some 23,000 people are involved in accidents that leave them brain-dead, but fewer than 3,000 of those tragedies result in organ donations. Surgical teams at organ transplantation centers are ready around the clock, every day of the year, to recover organs and transplant them. Why, then, are so few organs used?

"Can you imagine how difficult it is to go to the parents of a dying child and ask them to sign a legal paper giving away parts of that child to someone they don't even know?" one emergency room nurse asked. "Time is crucial. It has to be done immediately. And yet you have to convince them that the doctors and nurses have done everything in their power to keep their child alive. I understand how they feel. They've just heard the worst news they'll ever get, and an outsider is suddenly asking them to think about the lives of others."

There are those who do not participate in organ donation because their religion forbids it. The Orthodox Jewish religion, for example, does not allow burial of a disfigured or mutilated body in a consecrated[3] cemetery, and the loss of an organ is considered a disfigurement.

In many hospitals, a person called an organ procurement[4] coordinator or a transplant coordinator is responsible for asking the grieving families to donate organs and for matching them with those who need a specific organ. One coordinator, describing a typical situation, said, "On this job you run through all the emotions. It's very sad to ask for the donation, but when you follow it through and see how many people are helped, it's incredibly rewarding."

A coordinator at St. Luke's Medical Center in Chicago said that one morning she was called to the intensive care unit of a hospital because a 15-year-old boy had been declared clinically[5] brain-dead. He had been riding his bicycle when he was hit by a car, leaving him with extensive and irreversible brain damage. Although his parents were overcome with grief, they knew they did not want their son lingering on a respirator.

The boy was receiving oxygen from a ventilator that made his heart beat artificially. He could not breathe on his own, and he had no response to pain. Because in this situation the patient's chest is moving and his skin has good color and feels warm, it may be difficult

---

2. **dialysis:** process of removing liquid waste material from the blood; an activity that can be done by a machine when the kidney is diseased or injured
3. **consecrated:** made sacred or holy
4. **procurement:** process of obtaining something
5. **clinically:** based on direct observation of a patient, as in a hospital or clinic

The organs from a single donor can change the lives of many people.

would stop beating. They could choose to discontinue any life-support and simply wait for him to die. Or they could donate their son's organs for transplant while those organs were still being supplied with oxygen. The family chose to donate the organs because it was a way of turning a tragic death into a heroic event. Had they decided to allow their son to die slowly on the respirator, the organs in his body would have been useless.

Organs are *never* recovered from a body without the written consent of the family. Even if the patient had at some time signed a donor card or a "living will" indicating that he wanted to give his organs, the actual removal of the organs, in this country, does not take place without written permission. Next of kin who sign the consent form may even specify which organs may be taken. One family allowed all the organs to be used except their son's eyes. Requests of that kind are always honored.

In the case of the 15-year-old Chicago boy, the moment the parents signed the permission forms, the transplant coordinator put a well-rehearsed plan into action. First, she entered the weight, blood type, age, and

to believe the patient is really dead. Off the respirator, however, a brain-dead person would not be able to breathe and his heart would stop. No patient who has met the stringent criteria[6] of brain death has ever lived.

Brain death is not the same as a coma, in which a person's brain activity may be recorded. In total brain death, both the voluntary and involuntary responses stop working. Breathing is an involuntary function of the autonomic nervous system; you don't have to think about it. The voluntary nervous system controls conscious actions like muscular movement. In brain death, it's as though the main switch has been pulled.

The family of this boy faced three choices. They could keep their son on artificial life-support, but his body would quickly deteriorate and his heart soon

---

6. **stringent criteria:** strict guidelines

This helicopter helps an organ recovery team to transport organs as quickly as possible to people who need them. Notice the hand-held cooler that can be used to carry organs such as kidneys.

sex of the donor into a telephone computer system called NATCO 24-Alert Organ Sharing System. The North American Transplant Coordinators Organization created this computer program in 1983 at the University of Pittsburgh in order to match donors and recipients at any time, anywhere, with one phone call. If the organs can't be used locally, they are sent out. In a few minutes, the computer screen displayed which transplant centers in North America had people who needed this boy's organs. The coordinator made the necessary phone calls to alert the transplant teams from those centers and to schedule an operating room. The recovery of organs is carried out under the same careful, sterile[7] conditions used for any surgery.

The next step was ordered and disciplined. A highly trained surgical team of four from Yale University Hospital, scheduled to recover the liver, flew to Chicago where an ambulance met them for a fast ride to the hospital. A team of seven cardiac specialists from Loyola University in Chicago was flown by helicopter directly to the hospital grounds because every minute counts in recovering a heart. The team of seven surgeons from nearby Rush Medical Center drove to the hospital because the kidneys they would recover could be preserved longer than the other organs. Eye surgeons from the Illinois Eye Bank were scheduled last because the recovery of the corneas for transplant can be done

---

7. **sterile:** free of harmful organisms

after the patient is removed from the respirator. Corneas can be stored in a tissue bank for up to four days.

The coordinator arranged every detail so that each team's time in the operating room went smoothly and transportation from airport to hospital and back was as fast as possible. Most recovery teams have to take the first available commercial flight, but in some areas corporations donate a jet and crew for the team's use. Timing is crucial, especially for the recovery of heart and liver, which are stored in a "slush" solution of ice and water. Kidneys, with a longer preservation time, are usually delivered in a regular picnic cooler.

While all the organizing is going on, the nurses in the intensive care unit keep the brain-dead patient's vital signs[8] as stable as possible. With the respirator forcing oxygen into the lungs, the heart continues to pump the oxygenated blood to the organs, and the kidneys continue to get rid of the waste.

The American Council on Transplantation, formed in 1983, says that the shortage of donors is caused by people's not knowing about the need or being misinformed. They don't know how transplantation is done or how much it costs. The expense of transplantation is enormous, but it costs nothing to be a donor.

Because most patients who become donors arrive at the hospital in critical condition,[9] permission must come from family members. Until 1986, there was no way to require hospital officials to ask for organ donations. In the first states to pass "required request" legislation, California, Oregon, New York, and Connecticut, hospitals reported enormous increases in the number of donations.

Why sign a donor card and carry it in your wallet? The American Council on Transplantation suggests that anyone who signs a donor card should discuss the matter with family members because the card will serve as a reminder to them at the time of the person's death.

Transplant coordinators agree that most donor families have two things in common: generosity and sensitivity. They want to make something good come out of tragedy.

---

8. **vital signs:** measured indicators of life such as pulse rate, breathing rate, body temperature, and blood pressure
9. **critical condition:** state of being in danger of dying

From *Spare Parts for People*, by Margery and Howard Facklam

The AIDS epidemic that came to public notice in the 1980s has shown what can happen when people's immune defense systems stop working. Did you know the immune defense system can also cause problems by working too hard? Read to learn about the role the immune defense system can play in different people's lives.

Your Immune Defense System

Would you believe that lurking beneath the quiet surface of your body you have a ferocious army of defenders busily fighting grim life-or-death battles, night and day, to protect you from alien invaders?

This is not a science-fiction story. It's the truth. That protective army is your natural *immune defense system* (usually just called the *immune system*), and the scientific study of the way it works is known as *immunology.*

Your immune system began fighting for your life soon after you were born, and—if all goes well—it will continue fighting for you through your entire life. It keeps working whether you are sick or well, happy or sad, awake or asleep. When it doesn't work properly, you can become very ill. But as long as it protects you as it should, you remain healthy in the midst of terrible dangers.

Protects you from what? From an amazing variety of things in the world around you that don't belong inside your body. Your immune system's primary task is to keep you alive, and it does that job remarkably well. If you didn't have an immune system, you might have to live in a strange, artificial world like a little boy named David.

A Body Without Defenses

Not long ago David celebrated his tenth birthday, and for him that was something of a miracle. Soon after he was born, David was sealed inside a completely airtight, germ-free plastic incubator.[1] From then on, nothing from the world outside could be allowed to come into contact with him without first being carefully treated to make it germ-

---

1. **incubator:** chamber in which conditions are controlled to support life

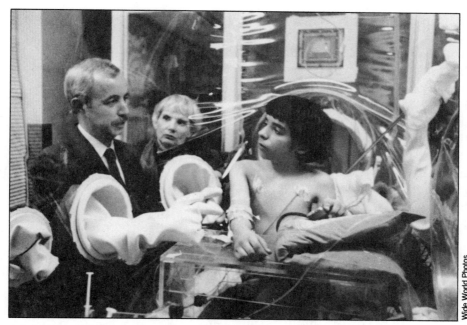

A doctor talks with David, who sits inside of his germ-free plastic unit.

free. He could not be allowed to touch another human being, not even his own parents. As he grew, he had to have larger and larger plastic "houses" in which to live. He could only go outside his germ-free cage by dressing in a plastic "space suit," like a moon-walking astronaut. On his tenth birthday his parents and friends were there to celebrate—but they all had to stay *outside* his plastic barrier.

Why couldn't David live like other people did? There was nothing wrong with the world around him, but there was something very wrong with David. While his body was developing before birth, an important part of David was left out—the immune defense system we spoke of earlier. He had no protective army inside him fighting to keep him alive—none at all.

Doctors spoke of David's rare disorder as *combined immuno deficiency disease*. All this meant was that David's body had no natural protection against the alien invaders—including the bacteria[2] and viruses[3]—that surround us on all sides. Nor was there any way at that time to supply David with the immune protection his body lacked. (Today a bone-marrow[4] transplant might have helped.) When immune protection isn't present naturally, there is usually just no substitute for it.

David's doctors knew what would happen to this boy if he were to go outside his germ-free plastic house

2. bacteria: single-celled microorganisms, some types of which can cause disease
3. viruses: tiny disease-causing units of genetic material inside protein coats that can reproduce themselves inside a living cell
4. bone marrow: substance inside bones that is important in forming blood cells that fight disease

without any immune protection and try to live like the rest of us. Very soon he would be sick with a cold, a sore throat, or an earache—and the illness would linger on and on. He would go from one infection to another in spite of antibiotics[5] or any other treatment, until finally one infection would become so severe that medicines wouldn't be able to control it and he would die. He might survive a couple of months or years outside his germ-free house, but not much longer. But having to live in a plastic cage forever was hardly much better. After careful thought, his doctors decided to try using medicines to build up an artificial immunity in David, and then released him to live in a germ-free room in his home. Unfortunately, it didn't work. Before his twelfth birthday, David died from a series of overwhelming infections. Today doctors hope that newly discovered treatments, including bone-marrow transplants, may someday help children like David overcome their immune deficiency, but so far there is still no effective treatment.

Fortunately, David's kind of immuno deficiency disease is extremely rare. Most people are born with perfectly normal, fully active immune systems that can work for them all their lives, and up until recently doctors seldom had to deal with immune-deficiency diseases. But now, since 1980, a terrible epidemic called AIDS (Acquired Immune Deficiency Syndrome) has been destroying the immune systems of thousands of people all over the world. AIDS is caused by a virus that invades the body and directly attacks the immune systems of formerly perfectly healthy

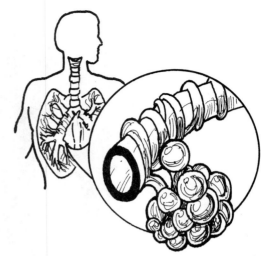

In normal lungs, air tubes are open and breath moves freely.

people. With their immune systems destroyed, victims of AIDS can die just as inexorably[6] as David did.

The Other Side of the Picture

Meanwhile, many people have problems not because they lack immune defenses, but because their immune systems are working a little too vigorously.

Mary Sue K. has such a problem. On an April morning every year she wakes up sneezing violently, her eyes red, her nose itching. For the next three weeks her nose will run constantly, her ears will itch, and she will sneeze and sneeze. A special antihistamine[7] medicine will clear up her symptoms for a few hours at a time, but they come back just as soon as the medicine wears off. Then about three weeks after they start, the symptoms go away all by themselves just as suddenly and mysteriously as they began.

5. **antibiotics:** substances that stop the growth of or kill certain microorganisms
6. **inexorably:** without a decrease in harshness
7. **antihistamine:** medicine that reduces swelling and other cold and allergy symptoms

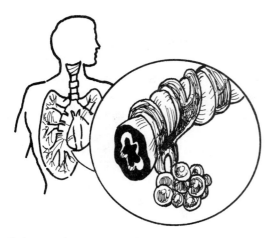

During an asthma attack, air tubes in the lungs squeeze shut, and breathing becomes difficult.

Mary Sue's doctor says that she has "hay fever," caused by an allergic reaction to maple tree pollen. (No other pollens seem to bother her.) During her attacks, the moist inner lining of her nose becomes clogged with a special kind of white blood cell[8] not normally present in such large numbers. This is a telltale sign that her immune system is fiercely *overreacting* to contact with an "alien invader"—the offending pollen—and that is exactly what an allergic reaction is. By starting a long series of injections in the middle of the winter to make her body less sensitive to the pollen, Mary Sue might avoid her hay fever attack the next spring, but she prefers just to take the antihistamines for relief until the pollen goes away and the symptoms disappear on their own.

Mary Sue's hay fever is mostly just a nuisance. She is one of millions of people who have minor allergic reactions to various foreign substances they come into contact with. But Roger M., a ninth-grader, has a more serious allergic problem. Since the age of six he has had

periodic attacks of *asthma,* a respiratory disease in which the tiny air tubes in the lungs squeeze shut, trapping air inside and forcing the victim to struggle and wheeze, trying to push the air out again. Roger's asthma attacks begin quite suddenly and without warning. First his chest begins to feel tight. A few moments later he is fighting for breath, coughing, and wheezing. Without the proper medicine, the attack might last all day or all night, leaving him exhausted. To prevent this, he must take pills every day and use a small medicinal inhaler to help keep his air tubules relaxed. This helps prevent attacks.

Asthma is not always caused by allergies alone; it can arise from many different sources. But allergies often play an important part. In Roger's case, his asthma results, in part, from an allergic reaction to the mold spores that are found in ordinary house dust. To help him avoid contact with these "alien invaders," Roger's bedroom is now fitted with special air filters, and everyone in his family works hard to keep dust from accumulating. His asthma attacks are never life-threatening, and they always go away sooner or later, but they are a thoroughly frightening and unpleasant health problem just the same. Unfortunately, Roger may have asthma for the rest of his life. His natural immune system is working so hard protecting him from a foreign substance—mold spores—that it actually makes him far sicker than the mold spores alone could possibly make him.

8. **white blood cell:** cell in the blood that defends against foreign matter

At age 13 Kathy D. had an even more frightening allergic problem. Kathy didn't think she was allergic to anything until one day at summer camp when she was stung by a bee—and thought she was going to die as a result of it. Right away her eyelids grew puffy, and huge, itchy bumps appeared all over her body. A few moments later her voice went hoarse, breathing became difficult, and she almost became unconscious. Fortunately, the camp nurse recognized what was happening and injected her with a medicine called Adrenalin to quiet the attack long enough to get her to a nearby hospital emergency room. There, other treatment restored Kathy's abnormally low blood pressure and soon put an end to her sudden and frightening attack. The doctor said she had suffered an *anaphylactic shock*—a sudden, massive overreaction of her body's immune system to an alien invader, in this case the venom from a bee sting. On rare occasions, people may have similar violent reactions to penicillin, horse serum, or other medicines. Fortunately, such severe reactions to bee stings aren't very common—most people have only a little harmless burning and swelling after a sting. But when it does occur, such a reaction can be very dangerous unless the proper medicine is available and quickly administered. Kathy now carries a "bee-sting kit" of emergency medicines wherever she goes. In addition, she is undergoing treatment to make her body less sensitive to bee venom so the next bee sting will not affect her so seriously.

In the last three cases, the body's immune system has been overdoing its job of protecting these young people against the invasion of relatively trivial foreign substances. Usually allergies are just a minor nuisance, but in some people they become serious health problems, and on occasion they might even threaten life. But in each case the same basic sequence of events has occurred. First, some foreign substance has found entry into the body. Next, in sharp response, the immune system has sprung into action against the invader and—in these cases—has done its job too well.

Obviously your immune system is a powerful weapon, absolutely necessary to keep you alive—yet it can be a two-edged sword. When it isn't working properly, people like David and thousands of AIDS victims get sick and die. When it does its job too well, people can also get sick.

But for most people, the immune system does far more good than harm. It is a very important and very complex part of the way your healthy body works to stay healthy. It has a real and vital purpose. And although many people experience annoying allergic reactions of one sort or another sometimes in their lives, the immune system mostly does its protective work quietly and unobtrusively[9]—and we survive because of it.

---

9. **unobtrusively:** unnoticed; without getting in the way

From *Your Immune Defense System*, by Alan E. Nourse, M.D.

Bees

What would it be like to have no choice at all about the kind of work you do? Bees don't have a choice. If a bee is born a worker bee, it must do the specific jobs of a worker bee its entire life. Read to learn about the few roles bees can play in a bee colony.

Insects[1] that live together are called *social insects*. Bees, termites, and ants are the best-known social insects.

The insect colony, or society as it is sometimes called, is much like a human society. The members live and work with others of the same kind. Each insect does his or her own job. They work together and divide the work among them. In our society, one might be a teacher, shoe salesman, mechanic, or doctor. No one does all the work himself. We are all somewhat dependent on others. In most human societies, the members are free to choose what kind of work they want to do. In the insect society, however, the insect has no such choice. It is born into a particular

---

1. Insects: small animals with no backbones, six legs, and bodies divided into three main sections

A close-up view of a bee's barbed stinger

class, or *caste*. It must remain in that caste for the rest of its life. If an insect is born as a worker, it will remain a worker. There is no way that the insect could change its caste.

Insects, unlike people, have no sense of the importance of the individual members of the society. When a bee hive is attacked, the bees drive off the attacker by stinging it. This kills the bees that do the stinging, but they never hesitate. They recognize only the importance of the hive.

In all societies, there must be a balance between the number of individuals and the number of different jobs. There cannot be too many individuals doing the same job. In the human society, people can learn different kinds of work. However, insect behavior is not learned. Each insect knows from birth what it must do. It cannot learn a new job. If there are too many for one job, the extras must die. There are no new ways of doing things. An insect society is the same today as it will be 200 years from now.

What Is the Bee Colony Like?

The bee colony is a very interesting and well-ordered one. There are three castes of bees: the *worker,* the *drone,* and the *queen.* The queen controls the reproduction of new bees in the hive. She lays eggs until she dies or is killed. She may lay as many as 3,000 eggs a day. She usually lives from 3 to 10 years. The total number of eggs that a queen bee lays in her lifetime may be in the millions.

The drone bees are all males. They have only one function in life—to mate with a queen. When a queen is ready to mate, she flies off and leaves the hive. The drones follow her. It is only the strongest of the drones that can catch the queen and mate with her. The rest of them become weak and die along the way. When a queen mates with a drone, she receives sperm cells which she stores in her body. These are all the sperm cells she will need to fertilize eggs for the rest of her life.

To the workers, then, is left the job of caring for the hive, raising young, and gathering food. As you might expect, the worker class is by far the largest. All of the workers are females. In a single hive, there may be only 100 drones, but there may be 60,000 workers. There is only one queen.

As the workers grow older, the jobs they do change. Newly hatched workers feed the queen and the young larvae.[2] This is no easy job, as a single larva may eat as many as 1,300 meals a day.

As the worker ages, wax glands grow on the underside of her abdomen. She scrapes this wax off with her legs and chews it. The wax is then used for building and repairing the hive.

Younger workers keep the hive clean and also protect it from enemies. A few other worker bees guard the entrance to the hive against dangerous enemies.

The bee's stinger is found at the rear of its abdomen. It has barbs on it much like those on a fish hook. These barbs keep it from being pulled out after it has been placed in a victim. Thus, the bee must leave behind a part of its abdomen, including the poison gland. Poison will still be pumped into the victim after the bee has flown away. The bee itself, however, will die. If the bee should sting another insect, though, its stinger is not pulled out, and the bee does not die.

About three weeks after they hatch, workers take on the job of food gathering. It is only the grown workers that gather pollen and nectar to make honey.

Pollen is stored on the bee's legs in special places called *pollen baskets*. To collect one load of pollen, a bee must visit from 50 to 1,000 flowers. During one summer, a hive may use as much as 100 pounds of

---

2. **larvae:** the wormlike young forms of insects that change to become the adults

pollen. This pollen contains great amounts of protein, which is needed by the young larvae.

Worker bees also collect a sugary liquid called *nectar* from flowers. The amount of sugar in the nectar depends on the type of flower it comes from. Sweet clover nectar may have as much as 60 percent sugar. The nectar is sucked up and stored in a special honey sac. To fill the honey sac, the bee visits over 1,000 flowers. To make a thimbleful of honey, 60 loads of nectar are needed. Some larger beehives may store as much as two pounds of honey per day.

Honey is made by evaporating, or drying, the nectar after it has been mixed with a liquid from the mouths of the bees. The nectar is passed back and forth between the bees and then placed in the cells[3] of the hive. The workers fan the nectar with their wings to speed evaporation.

Worker bees also have another job. That is the job of keeping the temperature in the hive at a certain level. When the temperature drops below 57 degrees, the bees gather in a ball and fan their wings rapidly. Inside the ball, the temperature remains at about 90 degrees. If, on the other hand, the temperature inside the hive is too high, the bees bring in water and evaporate it by fanning their wings. The drying of the water lowers the temperature in the hive.

How Do Bees Communicate?

Can bees communicate with one another? We have learned that they can, and the manner in which they do it is interesting. Their way of communicating is by dancing, rather than by sounds.

What type of things do bees communicate about? If a worker bee finds a good source of nectar, she may want to tell the others. In doing this, she must not only show where the nectar source is, but also how far it is from the hive.

A complicated dance by the worker gives all the information. If the nectar supply is close, less than 100 yards away, the worker does a circle dance. As she dances, she drops bits of nectar so that other bees will know what type of flower to look for. The speed of the dance tells how good the supply is. A very good supply will be shown by a very fast dance.

If the nectar is more than 100 yards away, the bee must not only show how far it is, but also the direction. If the nectar supply is far away, the

---

3. **cells:** small, hollow places

A bee gathering pollen

dance the bee does is different than that done for a nearby supply. This dance is a wagging dance, done in the form of a figure eight. The bee shows the distance by the speed of the dance and the wags of its abdomen. If the nectar supply is fairly close, the wagging is fast. Distant supplies are shown by a slower wagging.

Bees use the position of the sun in the sky to show the direction to the nectar supply. The direction in which the bee moves in the long part of the figure eight shows the direction of flight that must be followed. This is easy if the dance is done outside the hive. However, it is usually done inside. It is done on a vertical, or up and down, surface, rather than on a horizontal, or level, surface. On a vertical surface, straight up is the direction of the sun. A direction to the right of the sun would be shown by dancing to the right of straight up. Straight down would be away from the sun. This is the way in which bees are able to learn the distance and direction to a supply of nectar.

Bees also tell about places for a new hive. When the colony grows too large it produces a new queen and divides. One part goes with the new queen and the other part stays with the old queen. To find a new home, a "scout" bee goes out to look for a good spot. When it finds one, it returns to the hive and tells the other bees about it by dancing.

The speed of the dance tells how good the spot is. If another bee likes the spot, she, too, will dance for it. Finally, there is a decision as to the best spot. No vote is made by the queen. Everything is democratic, and all advertising is honest. A bee who at first advertised a poor spot will check the better spot. It will join in with the others if it likes the spot.

How Does the Queen Regulate the Colony?

The queen bee is able to regulate, or control, the size of the colony. She lays the eggs for the hive and can regulate the number of worker or drone bees to be hatched. There is only one queen for each hive. There will be no other queen unless the colony becomes too large or the queen dies.

But how can the queen control the caste of the new bees? She is able to control the number of males and females. The drones are all males, and the workers are all females. How is it possible, though, to have 600 times as many females as males? If you look at our human population, you will see that the number of males and females is about the same. The queen bee, however, can control the sex of a new bee. If she allows the egg to be fertilized, it will hatch as a female. If she chooses not to fertilize an egg, it will become a male. The queen bee is thus able to regulate the sex and caste of all new bees in the hive.

But what if another queen is needed? The queen lays a fertilized egg, just as she does for a worker female. It is the food that the growing larva eats that controls whether it hatches into a queen or remains a worker. Workers are immature, or not fully grown, females. They can never lay eggs.

What is the food of the queen bee? It is known as *royal jelly*. It is made by glands in the heads of workers. How do the workers know when to feed the royal jelly to a larva? The queen gives off a substance which rubs off on the workers as they care for her. For some reason, this substance keeps workers from making a new queen. Should the queen die, the workers will start feeding royal jelly to several larvae.

When the first of these new queens comes out from her queen cell, she kills all the other unhatched queens. In this way, she will be the only queen.

If the colony becomes too large, the queen no longer keeps the workers from making a new queen. Before the new queen hatches, the old queen flies off with a large number of workers to start a new hive. The old hive is left for the new queen.

From *Exploring and Understanding Insects*, by Barbara J. Collins

Unit 2: Physics

the science that deals with the properties and interrelationships of matter and energy

© 1953 M.C. Escher / Cordon Art - Baarn - Holland

What Physics Is, and How We Use It

Physics is the branch of science that deals with the relationships between physical objects and energy. The study of how things move is an important part of physics. How do you think discoveries in the field of physics have changed the way people live?

Asking Questions

The science of physics began when people started asking questions about the things they saw around them. To get examples of what is studied in physics, think of some of the questions that you might ask when you spend a day at the seashore.

At the beginning of the day you find the sun low in the eastern part of the sky. As the day passes, the sun rises until it is almost overhead. Then it becomes lower again as it moves on to the west. Why does the sun seem to move across the sky? Why does it repeat its journey across the sky every day?

The beach and the water nearby are flooded with light that comes from the sun. What makes the light in the sun? How does it cross the space that is between us and the sun? Why is the light brighter at the beach than it is in a city street or in a field in the country?

In the early morning the sand on the beach feels cool. As the sun shines on the sand, the sand becomes hot. What is

heat? How does the sunlight make the sand hot? Why does the sand cool off again at night?

As you sit in the sunshine, if your skin is light it will turn red or tan. If you stay in the sunlight too long you may get a painful sunburn. What makes the sunburn?

The people around you wear bathing suits of many different colors. What is color? What makes the different colors that you see?

Most of the grains of sand on the beach are white or yellow or pink. Scattered among these light grains are some black ones. If you hold a magnet close to the sand, some of the black grains jump up to the magnet. What makes them jump?

At the edge of the beach, where the water meets the land, there is movement all the time. Waves roll in, one after the other, and crash on the beach with a roar. What are waves? What makes them? What causes the sound that they make?

When you come ashore after a swim, your skin and your bathing suit are wet. Why does the water stick to them? As you sit on the beach, you feel a wind blowing in from the sea. What makes the wind? Why does your wet skin feel cool as the wind blows over it? After a while your skin and your bathing suit become dry. What happened to the water that was on them when they were wet?

Scattered along the beach are pieces of driftwood washed ashore by the waves. Sometimes even a big heavy log is carried ashore by the water. Why does a heavy log float in the water? If you try to raise a big log by grasping it at the middle, you will find it hard to lift. But if you grasp the log at one end, you will find it easier to raise that end off the ground. Why is it easier to raise one end than it is to raise the whole log?

Late in the afternoon, clouds may appear in the sky. Where did they come from? On some days it may begin to rain. What makes the rain? Why do the

A telescope brings distant objects into view.

crashing waves to your ears. When you stand on the beach, heat moves from the hot sand into your feet. Even colors, like red and blue, arise out of a kind of movement.

There is a special word for things that exist and take up space. We call them *matter*. Physics is the study of the relationships between matter and energy. Many of these relationships involve motion. The physicist asks, "What is matter made of? What are the different kinds of motion? What are the laws governing the motion of matter?"

raindrops fall to the ground? If there is a thunderstorm you may see flashes of lightning. Then you will leave the beach to find shelter indoors, because it is not safe to be on a beach when there is lightning. What is lightning? What makes it? Why is it so dangerous?

On a clear night, after the sun has set, you will see stars arranged in fixed patterns that you can recognize night after night. You will also see the moon and some planets seeming to move about among the stars. What makes them move?

Things that Move

All of these questions are about things that really exist, take up space, and move. The sun and the planets move about in the sky. Light from the sun moves through space to reach us. The water in the waves moves up and down on the beach. The end of a log moves up when you lift it. Sound moves from the

Finding Answers

The job of the physicist is to find answers to these questions. To understand the motions of matter, he *observes* them. He looks at things, listens to them, and feels them. In order to observe carefully, he always *measures*. Sometimes he performs *experiments* in which he makes things happen. He may roll a ball down a slope, swing a pendulum,[1] or smash atoms. In every experiment he purposely makes some changes in things to see what other changes happen as a result.

After he has gathered many facts about the things he has observed, the physicist forms a mental picture of how the facts are related to each other. This mental picture is called a *theory*. A theory is good if it explains many facts in a simple way. As the physicist gathers more facts he also makes up better theories.

---

1. pendulum: an object or a weight hung from a fixed point and free to swing back and forth, acting under the influence of gravity

The physicist uses old knowledge to help him gather new knowledge. The old knowledge helps him build instruments with which he can see and measure things better. He uses telescopes and cameras in order to see better than he would if he used his eyes alone. He uses microphones and amplifiers in order to hear better than he would if he used his ears alone. He uses bolometers to help him feel and measure heat. He uses barometers to help him feel and measure pressure. In a modern physics laboratory the physicist uses many complicated instruments to observe and measure happenings.

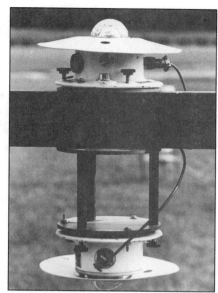

A bolometer is a very sensitive type of thermometer.

Using the Answers

After the physicist helps us understand how things move, we can often make them move in useful ways. We put the knowledge of the physicist to

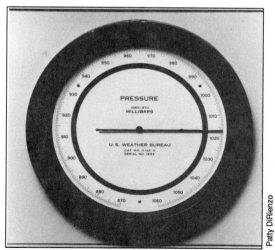

A barometer measures air pressure.

work for us through inventions that make our work lighter, increase our comfort, and allow us to do things that we could not do before.

We make stoves to cook our food and radiators to heat our homes. We make electric lamps to give us light and electric motors to turn the machines in our factories. We make radio and television transmitters that change sounds and pictures into electrical signals and then send them across great distances to receivers. We make locomotives and automobiles to carry us and our goods over the ground. We make ships that cross the ocean and airplanes that fly through the air. We smash the atom to unlock its hidden energy. We also make rockets that fly out of the earth's atmosphere and go to the moon or the planets Venus and Mars.

From *The Wonders of Physics*, by Irving Adler

Shopping Cart

Oklahoma City supermarket operator Sylvan N. Goldman watched, day after day, as customers struggled to carry all their purchases.

He decided to come up with a better way. Working in his small office one night in 1936, he placed together two small folding chairs.

"Inspiration hit me right between the eyes!" he later said. He figured out that by fastening the chairs together, putting wheels under them, and placing a basket on top of each seat, he had developed the shopping cart.

In Goldman's perfected model, steel replaced wood. His first metal cart is on permanent display at the Smithsonian Institute in Washington, D.C.

Traffic Light

Even during the horse and buggy days, traffic in big cities was often heavy. Police officers had to be stationed full time directing traffic at busy intersections.

And with the coming of automobiles, the situation got even worse.

Police officer William Potts of Detroit, Michigan, decided to do something about the problem. What he had in mind was figuring out a way to adapt railroad signals for street use.

The railroads were already utilizing automatic controls. But railroad traffic traveled along parallel[2] lines. Street traffic traveled at right angles.[3]

Potts used red, amber, and green railroad lights and about $37 worth of wire and electrical controls to make the world's first traffic light.

It was installed in 1920 on the corner of Woodward and Michigan Avenues in Detroit.

Within a year, Detroit had installed a total of 15 of the new automatic lights. Today, there are over 125,000 throughout the United States.

From *Why Didn't I Think of That?* by Webb Garrison

2. **parallel:** extending alongside and always at an equal distance from one another; side by side
3. **right angles:** resulting from the meeting and crossing of lines as in a plus sign (+); 90° angles

Eureka!
I Found It!

Do you know why a 10-ton ship floats in the sea, but a tiny pebble sinks to the bottom? Archimedes, a scientist in ancient Greece, was curious about why some things float and other things sink. Read about the unusual way he came up with the answer.

An oceangoing ship weighs hundreds or even thousands of tons. Yet it can float on water. How is that possible? The answer begins with one of the oldest and most famous stories in the history of science.

Let's imagine an experiment. You decide to take a bath, and so you turn on the water and fill the tub to the very top. Then, with the tub filled just to overflowing, you step in and sit down.

Even without trying, you know exactly what will happen. In fact, you'd better not try it, unless you want to do a lot of mopping up afterward! When you get into the tub, gallons of water will pour onto the floor.

According to an ancient story, this is just what happened to the Greek scientist Archimedes more than 2,200 years ago. Archimedes sat down in an overly full bathtub, and water flooded over the sides. Seeing the water overflow gave Archimedes a brilliant idea. He was so excited about his new idea that he jumped out of the tub. Forgetting to put on his clothes, he ran through the streets shouting, "Eureka!" which means *I found it!*

Archimedes had been thinking about why some things float while others sink. It couldn't be just a matter of weight. Greek ships were very heavy, and yet they floated. But even a tiny pebble sinks right to the bottom of the sea.

What Archimedes found in his bathtub was the law of buoyancy.[1] This is now usually known as Archimedes' Principle in his honor. Archimedes' Principle says: Any floating object pushes aside, or *displaces,* an amount of water equal to its own weight. If a boat weighs 500 pounds, it must displace 500 pounds of water in order to float.

Imagine a boat pushing a "hole" into the water. If you measured the amount of water it would take to fill that hole, it would weigh just as much as the boat itself. A boat that weighs 100 tons must push aside 100 tons of water to float.

If you measure carefully, you will be able to see this law at work in the following demonstration.

Place an aluminum pie plate on a sensitive scale. Weigh it and record its weight. Now find an object that will float, like a block of wood, weigh it, and write down its weight.

Put the pie plate back on the scale. Place an empty can or wide-mouthed jar in the center of the plate. Carefully fill the jar with water to the very top. The water should be ready to overflow if you add just one more drop.

Now gently lower the block of wood into the can of water until it floats by itself. Some of the water in the can will overflow as the block pushes it out of the can. That's exactly what should happen.

After the wood is floating in the can, carefully lift the whole can, with the wood and water, out of the pie plate. Pick up the can very gently so that you don't spill any more water out of it.

Now weigh the pie plate with the overflow water in it. Subtract the weight of the pie plate itself. That will give you the weight of the water that the block of wood pushed out of the can.

---

1. buoyancy: the tendency of an object to float or the power of a liquid or gas to cause an object to rise in or through it

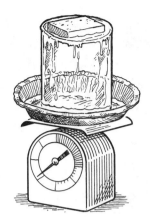

Using a scale, pie plate, and jar, you can demonstrate Archimedes' Principle.

Total weight of water and pan
− Weight of pan
───────────────────────────
Weight of water in pan

Compare the weight of the water in the pan to the weight of the block of wood. They should be equal. The water that the floating object displaces weighs just as much as the object itself. That's Archimedes' Principle.

Archimedes' Principle is true for any object, in any situation. That's why it's considered a law. If an object can displace its own weight in water, it will float. If it's too heavy or dense to displace its own weight, it will sink.

Try the same experiment using a rock instead of a block of wood. The rock will sink to the bottom. As it does, it will push some of the water out of the jar and into the pie plate. Compare the weight of the rock with the weight of the water it displaced. You should discover that the rock weighs more than the water in the pan. The rock wasn't able to displace its own weight in water, and so it sank.

Archimedes' Principle can be described in another way: If an object is less dense than water, it will float. If it is denser than water, it will sink.

Two different objects can be exactly the same size (or volume), but one can be much heavier than the other. A brick and a block of plastic foam may be exactly the same size. But when you compare their weights, the brick is much heavier. The brick has much greater *density*.

The material an object is made of has a lot to do with whether or not it will float. But, as you might guess from the way boats are designed, so does an object's shape. Here's another experiment to show how true that is.

Tear off two equal-sized sheets of aluminum foil. Fold one into the shape of a canoe. Crush the other one into a small ball, squeezing it as tightly as you can.

Now place both pieces of foil in a container of water. The ball sinks right to the bottom. As long as it doesn't fill with water, the "canoe" should float. Because of its shape, the canoe can displace its own weight of water, and so it floats. The densely packed ball cannot displace enough water, and so it sinks.

A submarine is a very special kind of boat. It uses Archimedes' Principle very precisely to either sink or float. A submarine has several ballast[2] tanks in its hull. When these tanks are filled with water, the submarine weighs more than the water it displaces. It sinks toward the bottom.

When the captain wants to float to the surface, he forces the water out of the tanks with compressed air. This makes the submarine lighter. It then displaces more than its own weight of water, and so it rises toward the surface.

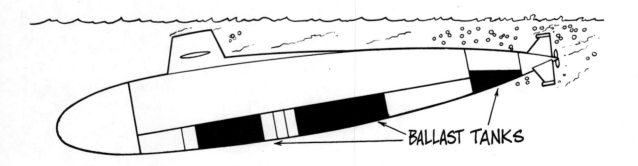

BALLAST TANKS

2. ballast: anything used to steady a person or thing

To keep the submarine at one certain depth, the captain allows just enough water in the tanks to give the submarine *neutral buoyancy*. That means that the ship weighs exactly as much as the water it displaces. It stays just where it is, neither rising nor sinking.

Archimedes' Principle doesn't apply just to objects floating in water. It's true for any liquid or gas.

Helium is less dense than air. A helium-filled balloon will rise in the air because it displaces more than its own weight.

A balloon filled with the heavy gas xenon will quickly sink to the ground. It weighs much more than an equal volume of air. And a heavy bar of steel will float gently on the surface of a pool of mercury, an even denser liquid metal.

Archimedes made many other noteworthy contributions to science and technology. He invented a new type of water pump. He began the science of mechanics, the study of how objects move. He explained how to use levers to move heavy burdens. Although he hated war, he invented new weapons to help the Greeks defend themselves against their enemies. But the contribution for which he is best remembered still bears his name. Eureka!

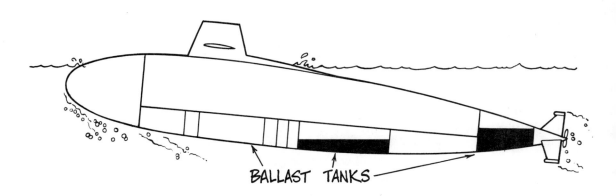

BALLAST TANKS

From *Secrets of the Universe*, by Paul Fleisher

Egg Float

Things you will need:
1 fresh egg, cooked or uncooked
Glass of water, almost full
Teaspoon
Salt

What to do:
Gently put the egg into the almost-full glass of water. The egg sinks, right? Now pour in two heaping teaspoons of salt and stir it around the egg. Does anything happen to the egg? Pour in two more teaspoons of salt. What happens? Add salt until the egg changes its location in the glass.

Physics at work:
The egg sinks at first because it weighs more than the fresh water it displaces. However, salt water is heavier than fresh water. When the water becomes salty enough, the salt water displaced by the egg weighs more than the egg—and the egg floats to the top.

At the Water's Edge

Things you will need:
Eyedropper
Large glass of water filled to the brim
Smaller glass of water

What to do:
Fill the eyedropper from the smaller glass. Use it to add water one drop at a time to the large glass. Even after the large glass looks full, you should be able to add many more drops. As you add water, watch it rise over the top but not overflow.

Physics at work:
Surface tension forms a tight skin over the top surface of the water. As you keep adding water, the skin stretches, just like the surface of a water balloon. But surface tension isn't strong. If you add too much water, the skin will break.

From *Fun with Physics*, by Susan McGrath

Thermometers

Comstock

Comstock

Comstock

Have you ever noticed that temperatures are often given twice, in C degrees and in F degrees? What do the letters mean? In this selection, you'll read about two scales used to measure temperature and also about how different thermometers work.

Thermometers measure temperature—that is, how hot or cold something is. It can be the temperature of objects, of liquids, or of the air in a room.

You might have seen the simplest type of thermometer hanging on the wall of a room. It consists of a sealed glass tube with a bulb—a wider part—at one end. The bulb is filled with a liquid, which comes part of the way up the tube. The liquid may be mercury, which is a silvery color, or alcohol that has been colored red.

Nearly all materials expand—get larger—when they are heated. Mercury and alcohol expand a great deal. The higher the temperature, the farther the liquid in a thermometer rises up the tube. You see which marking on the glass the liquid has reached, and this tells you the temperature.

There are two different ways of marking temperatures on a thermometer. One is called the *Fahrenheit* scale, after its inventor, Gabriel Fahrenheit, an eighteenth-century German scientist. On this scale, the temperature at which water freezes—its freezing point—is 32 degrees. This is written as 32° F. The temperature at which water boils—its boiling point—is 212° F.

The other scale that you will see on a thermometer is called the *centigrade* or *Celsius* scale. Anders Celsius was an eighteenth-century Swedish scientist. *Centigrade* means *having a hundred steps*. On the centigrade scale, the freezing point of water is zero degrees, written as 0° C. The boiling point is 100 degrees, or 100° C. You will often see the Fahrenheit scale marked along one side of a thermometer and the centigrade scale marked along the other.

A doctor uses a special kind of mercury thermometer. It is made so that when you take the thermometer out of your mouth, the mercury stays up in the tube—it does not immediately begin to fall back to show room temperature. This gives the doctor time to see what your temperature is. Afterwards he shakes the thermometer to force the mercury down.

Another kind of thermometer, often used in greenhouses, has two little markers inside the tube. One is pushed upwards as the mercury rises, but is left behind when it falls. At the end of the day it shows the highest temperature reached. The other marker is pushed downwards when the mercury falls, and is left behind when it rises. So at the end of the night it shows the lowest temperature reached. This is important to a gardener, who wants to be sure that plants are not being damaged by too much heat or cold.

Alcohol boils at a much lower temperature than water, so an alcohol thermometer cannot be used to measure the temperature of water that is almost boiling. A mercury thermometer can be used up to about 300° C (570° F). But above that temperature the glass becomes soft and the mercury is close to boiling. Scientists and engineers have to use special kinds of thermometers to measure very high temperatures.

From *How Everyday Things Work*, by Chris Cooper and Tony Osman

Gift

from the Sun

....

Why do you think the sun is important to life on earth? What do you think would happen if there were no sun? Read to learn what precious gift we get from this powerful star, the center of our solar system.

Hot water and steam rise from the geyser Old Faithful in Yellowstone National Park, Wyoming.

Tony Stone Worldwide

Energy

Energy is one of the mysteries at the heart of nature. Even at our present advanced stage of science, we still cannot say exactly what it is, any more than we can see the breeze. But we can feel the breeze and watch its effects as it blows up a swirl of leaves or dust along the way, and we can also watch the effects of energy and see what rules it follows as it shifts from one form to another.

We can also describe energy. It is the capacity to do work, and *energy output* is the type and amount of energy used to get the work done. The muscle power you use to pull on your socks, the blowing wind that

moves a flying kite, and the fire that roasts hot dogs at a barbecue are a few examples of energy output. And, as might be expected, the more energy applied, the more work can be completed. Ten farmers working by hand can plant more seeds in a day than one farmer alone. Or the one farmer can multiply his energy by using a planting machine instead of depending only on his muscle power.

For countless centuries, people have been tackling the problem of multiplying energy. The history of human success—from humans who lived the way other animals do to humans who became masters of nature—lies in the discovery of how to master and use energy. Little by little, humans have piled up a mountain of discoveries, climbing as they went along, each step leading to the next. In fact, inventors and other science thinkers might almost be a group of mountain climbers, held together by lengths of time rather than lengths of rope.

During most of human history, this "mountain slope" was almost level, then it gradually curved upward and suddenly became very steep about 200 years ago when steam power, a new human-made energy source, was first used to turn the wheels of factories and railroad engines. Since that time, one new discovery has led to another faster and faster.

To see how sharply the mountain slope of energy output has been rising in the last 100 years, you need only look around your house. Imagine giving up all the things in the house that didn't exist a century ago; you'd have to go without electric light, a refrigerator, air conditioning, radio, television, telephone, and record player. There would

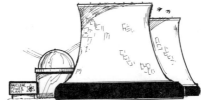

be no nylon stockings or plastic toys, and of course you couldn't travel by car or airplane. Life would be entirely different.

From human muscle power, our oldest energy source, to the newer ones like electricity, all the forms of energy can be talked about in terms of heat and motion. Heat may be partly changed to motion, as when the heat of the gas flame under the kettle first causes air bubbles to rise in the water and then sends jets of steam moving out of the kettle spout. Motion, in return, may be changed to heat; rubbing two sticks together in a certain way is a very ancient method of making enough heat to produce a spark that will light the fire.

But just as fire is a form of heat and running water is a form of motion, so heat and motion are forms of energy, not energy itself.

We have learned that energy and matter—the stuff all things are made of—are twins like heat and motion and that one can be changed to the other. Humankind has learned it to the sorrow of millions, by exploding atom bombs that changed a tiny amount of innocent atomic matter into a nightmare of flaming energy. Saying that energy and matter are twin forms of nature's great mystery is saying quite a lot, but does not explain the essence of what energy *is*. We must admit that we do not know and perhaps never shall.

We can, however, explain where the earth's energy comes from.

Strange as it may seem, the energy you use when you pull on your socks, the energy of burning gas that makes water boil, the energy of water flowing down a hillside, and nearly all the other energy we have used to make ourselves masters of our world can be traced to one source: the sun.

Sun

All our basic energy sources, except the very newest ones like atom-splitting, derive from the sun.

The sun's heat serves as the energy source, or "motor," for the earth's water cycle. In the same way that the heat of the stove causes steam to rise from the kettle spout, the heat of the sun draws up water from the earth in the form of vapor, or gas. You can't watch water vapor rising because it is as invisible as the air itself, but the sun draws up 16 million tons of water vapor every second from the earth's oceans, lakes, and streams.

This water vapor rises until it reaches a level where the air grows cooler. There it condenses into drops of moisture we see as clouds and finally falls to earth again in the form of rain or snow, filtering underground in many places. Much of this underground water comes out on the surface again; even an immense river like the Mississippi begins as a series of springs that gradually flow together.

The rivers flow back to the oceans, thus returning the water to its starting point to be picked up once again by the sun's heat. It is the motion of the water on the way back to the ocean that gives us our water power, the power turning many of the dynamos[1] that produce the electricity we depend on for so many things in our daily lives. A visit to the Grand Canyon makes the great force of running water very clear: the moving water of the Colorado River had enough energy to carve out one of the most astounding gorges in the world—a mile deep and, in some places, more than 15 miles wide.

While the sun's heat keeps the waters of the earth moving on their endless rounds, the sun's light provides the fuel for another energy cycle. All our food, the energy source for people and animals to grow and use their muscle power, goes back to sunlight. With the help of sunlight, plants can perform the magic of creating life, changing nonliving substances—water and the carbon dioxide gas in air—into living cells. This remarkable change supplies the fuel that all living, or animate, energy depends on.

---

1. **dynamos:** generators; machines that change mechanical energy into electrical energy

The Colorado River has been forming the Grand Canyon's awesome landscape for about six million years.

Plants make the basic food, some animals eat plants, and others eat the plant-eaters: a bug in the water nibbles on a green leaf, the fish snaps up the bug, and the fisherman catches the fish for dinner. With every bite of food we take, we are actually eating sunlight.

We not only eat sunlight but we burn it. When a piece of wood is put into the fire, it will yield energy in the form of heat; this energy was originally sunlight stored up by the tree as carbon compounds.[2] Nor is wood the only fuel that gets its store of energy from sunlight. The veins of coal that we mine today were living plants many millions of years ago—great leafy ferns, as big as trees, that could have shaded a huge dinosaur. Great amounts of pressure and heat as the earth's surface shifted through the ages compressed the remains of these plants into the coal now used as a key energy source. The earth's oil and natural gas supplies have the same kind of history. As with coal and wood, sunlight is what we are really burning when we use them.

We are also finding new ways to make direct use of the sun's heat energy in solar batteries or by means of mirrors that concentrate the heat to do work formerly done by other heat sources, work like separating the salt from sea water.

---

2. carbon compounds: substances made up of the element carbon in combination with other types of elements; carbon compounds make up the living tissue of all plants and animals.

A little of our energy comes from the earth itself. Unlike what its name suggests, for example, the island country of Iceland has enough hot springs welling up from the ground to keep many people there supplied with hot water and central heat in their houses. In a few other places on earth, where sea tides may rise and fall many feet every day, the energy of this moving water has been captured to turn engines that make electric power.

Very recently, we have discovered still another energy source, the atom, that does not depend on the sun. Though atoms are so small that they cannot be seen even under a powerful microscope, they consist of still smaller particles held together by strong bonds, like magnets pulling at each other. When the invisible parts of certain atom centers, or nuclei, can be made to fly apart, an amazing amount of energy is released. Properly controlled, the energy of atom-splitting or *atomic fission,* as it is called, can be used like water power to make electricity or, in some cases, to run boats or factories.

Another process known as *atomic fusion* releases even more energy. In a way, fusion is almost the opposite of splitting atoms apart, because it brings loose parts of atoms together to create new ones. So far, humankind has learned to use fusion only in fierce bombs that can destroy us all; maybe someday we will learn to control its fury. Inside the sun, where temperatures are unbelievably hot, the process of atomic fusion is happening all the time to produce the vast supply of energy that the sun throws all around itself, beaming it out into space in every direction.

Here's how much energy the sun has to give away. A *horsepower,* the term used to measure the energy of many engines, describes the amount of energy needed to lift 550 pounds of weight one foot in one second. Every second more than 1.5 million billion horsepower of energy reach the earth's surface from the sun—that means the number 1.5 with 14 zeroes after it: 1,500,000,000,000,000 horsepower. And that number is one part in 40 million—40,000,000—of what the sun is sending out. If you multiply those two numbers together, you'll have some idea of the sun's power to release energy.

From *Gift from the Sun: The Mastering of Energy,* by Margaret Cooper

Unit 3: Chemistry

*the science that deals with the study of
substances and the changes they undergo*

COMPOSITION IN CLAY, LEAVES, AND WAX, Gerald N. Bates, 1990, Private Collection

Did you know that you can change the ingredients in a cookie recipe on purpose to get just the taste or texture you want? It only takes a little "kitchen chemistry." (If you don't bake, share this selection with someone who does—then ask them to let you taste the results!)

Patty DiRienzo

How They Crumble

Most people don't have a clue to what makes a cookie crumble.

Americans love to eat cookies and they love to make them, but all too often their ideas about why one cookie is crisp and another is dry are half-baked.

It's because of the dough.

Cookies can be made in a mind-boggling array of shapes, sizes, textures, and flavors, but most cookies begin as a dough. (The exceptions are meringues, macaroons, unbaked varieties such as rum balls, and cake-like cookies such as madeleines, which all begin as batters.)

Basically, cookie dough is a combination of fat, sugar, flour, leavening, and moisture, such as egg. Changing the proportion of any basic ingredient also changes the texture of the dough and changes the cookie's character. Little variations make the difference between a great chocolate chip cookie and a good one. Large variations make bigger differences—like making oatmeal cookies crisp and peanut butter cookies crumbly.

Understanding how each ingredient affects the dough is the first defense against cookie catastrophes. It's also the best guarantee that every batch will emerge from the oven tasting like blue-ribbon winners in a country fair. Here's a crash course in cookie chemistry:

Butter, margarine, or shortening

All doughs begin with some type of fat. Recipes usually call for butter, unsalted butter, margarine, solid

Some basic cookie ingredients

shortening, or lard. Generally, all are interchangeable.

However, each produces slightly different results. Butter improves a cookie's flavor. Butter cookies also are crisper-textured, which is a bonus for types such as spritzes or wafers, but not necessarily a desirable trait in chocolate chips or thumbprint cookies. Solid shortening creates soft, spongy cookies that stay soft for a long time but have little taste. Lard creates flaky, slightly dry-textured cookies.

For many cookies, a combination of butter and margarine produces the best of both worlds. Margarine makes the cookie hold its shape, and butter gives it a distinctive, buttery flavor.

Most recipes begin with instructions to cream the butter, margarine, or shortening. This softens it and beats in air. The more air that is beaten into the fat, the lighter and fluffier the cookie will be.

However, there is a danger of overbeating—especially in warm, humid weather. If the fat becomes too warm and soft, the dough loses its airiness and becomes greasy. The baked cookies are flat and flabby. Chilling the dough before the cookies are formed and baked helps them retain their shape.

Avoid baking with whipped or diet margarine and whipped butter because they contain too high a proportion of water. And never substitute liquid oil in a recipe that calls for a solid fat.

Sugar and other sweeteners

Sugar not only sweetens the dough, but makes it tender. However, adding more sugar than a recipe calls for creates cookies that are brittle and glassy around the edges.

Most cookies call for granulated white sugar, but light or dark brown sugar can be substituted in most recipes. Brown sugars contain molasses, which gives the cookies a slightly richer flavor, darker color, and moister texture.

Honey or molasses can be used alone or in conjunction with white or brown sugar. Honey has a distinctive flavor and creates a chewy, moist texture. When substituting honey for sugar, use one-third less honey and cut back on other liquids in the recipe.

Molasses has a strong flavor, which is usually better tempered with other sweeteners. All-molasses cookies tend to be tough, hard, and dark.

Some recipes for chocolate-chip or spice cookies call for a small amount of corn syrup. Corn syrup produces a chewy cookie with a crisp exterior.

All sweeteners should be creamed with the fat. Creaming dissolves sugar. When the mixture is fluffy and soft, begin adding eggs and other liquids.

Eggs

The protein in eggs binds the dough together, and the moisture adds liquid. Cookies that don't contain any egg, such as shortbread, tend to be fragile and crumbly. Cookies that contain lots of eggs, such as brownies and bars, tend to be puffy and cake-like.

When recipes call for eggs, they usually mean the grade-A large variety. The eggs are beaten into the butter-and-sugar mixture one at a time to keep the creamed mixture fluffy and to beat in air. Fresh eggs at room temperature hold the most air.

Eggs seldom need to be beaten before they are added.

Leavening

In many cookie recipes, baking powder or baking soda provides puffiness. Without this leavening, the cookies would be hard and dry instead of light and flaky. Adding leavening is another way of incorporating air into the dough.

Baking powder contains an alkali[1] and an acid[2] that react when they get wet. The reaction forms carbon dioxide gas, which expands in the hot oven and fills the cookie with tiny air pockets. The pockets remain after the cookie is baked, creating light, tender cookies.

Double-acting baking powder is the most common leavening. It starts to react as soon as it comes in contact with moisture, though the majority of the leavening action occurs in heat. This double action ensures that baking powder is

---

1. **alkali:** a substance that, when dissolved in water, makes an acid in the water inactive
2. **acid:** a substance that, when dissolved in water, makes an alkali in the water inactive

effective even if the cookies aren't baked immediately. Doughs made with double-acting baking powder can be refrigerated or frozen.

Some recipes call for a small amount of baking soda in addition to baking powder. In most cases, baking soda is used in recipes that contain an additional acid, such as buttermilk, sour cream, yogurt, or molasses. However, baking soda starts to produce gas as soon as it is wet, so baking-soda cookies should be baked immediately.

Flours, oats, and grains

Flour is the foundation of the cookie, but the flavor should never be apparent when you taste the baked cookie. Cookies with too much flour have a pasty taste and a tough, dry texture.

Most recipes call for all-purpose flour, which is a mixture of soft, low-gluten[3] wheat and hard, high-gluten wheat. The combination gives the flour just enough gluten to produce light, tender cookies without making them elastic like bread.

Some recipes specify using other types of flour, such as whole wheat or cake flour. Whole wheat is more nutritious and nutty-tasting than all-purpose flour because it includes bran[4] and germ.[5] However, too much bran and germ can make the cookies heavy and dry. Even whole-wheat cookies should contain at least 1/4 cup of all-purpose flour.

Cake flour is made from very finely milled, low-gluten wheat. It produces the lightest, most tender results. Cake flour is appropriate to use in cookies that undergo a lot of handling, such as those formed by rolling the dough.

Regardless of the type used, flour should be added last and mixed as little as possible. Overmixing the flour forces air out of the dough and creates tough, hard cookies.

Few cookie recipes call for sifting the flour, but it should be carefully measured. For accuracy, spoon flour lightly into the appropriate-size measuring cup and scrape away the excess with the back of a knife.

Regular or quick-cooking oats are nutritious and delicious in cookies. Regular oats make heartier, more granola-like cookies; quick-cooking oats produce more delicate results. Avoid using instant oatmeal as an ingredient because it is powdery and may make the cookies dry.

Adding different grains and flours, such as soy, bran, cornmeal, or millet, gives cookies a nutritional boost as well as a different flavor and texture. However, too much can make the dough dry and crumbly.

Flavorings and other goodies

Vanilla and almond extract, spices, orange and lemon peel, coconut, chocolate, dried fruits, and nuts are a few

---

3. **low-gluten:** having a limited amount of the tough, sticky, elastic substance in flour
4. **bran:** the outer covering of grains, such as wheat and rye, used in cereal and bread
5. **germ:** seed; embryo of the wheat kernel

ingredients that add complexity and flavor to cookie doughs. How much is enough is a matter of personal taste.

Generally, doughs with lots of flavorings, nuts, chips, and chunks should be refrigerated after they are mixed. The cookies hold their shape better, and the dough doesn't become overmixed.

Chocolate Peanut Butter Cookies

Preparation time: 20 minutes
Cooking time: 10 to 12 minutes
Yield: About 3 dozen

8	ounces semisweet chocolate
1/2	cup (1 stick) unsalted butter
1 1/2	cups all-purpose flour
1/2	teaspoon baking powder
1/2	teaspoon salt
2	eggs
3/4	cup sugar
1 1/2	teaspoons vanilla
8	peanut butter cups, such as Reese's or other candies

1. Heat oven to 350°F. Have ungreased baking sheets ready.

2. Melt chocolate with butter in a microwave oven or in top of a double boiler. Set aside to cool slightly. Stir flour, baking powder, and salt together.

3. Beat eggs, sugar, and vanilla with electric mixer until light and fluffy. Add cooled chocolate and mix well. Stop mixer and add dry ingredients. Mix just until combined. Cut peanut butter cups into chunks and gently fold into batter.

4. Drop by large spoonfuls onto baking sheets. Bake until set, 10 to 12 minutes. Cool on baking sheets for 1 minute, then transfer to a wire rack to cool completely.

Chocolate-dipped Shortbread Fingers

Preparation time: 25 minutes
Cooking time: 12 to 14 minutes
Yield: About 5 dozen

1	cup (2 sticks) plus 1 tablespoon unsalted butter, softened
1/2	cup confectioners' sugar
2	teaspoons vanilla
	a pinch of salt
2 1/2	cups cake flour
6	ounces semi-sweet chocolate
2/3	cup chopped pecans or pistachio nuts

1. Heat oven to 350°F. Have ungreased baking sheets ready.

2. With an electric mixer, cream 1 cup of the butter with sugar, vanilla, and salt until light and fluffy. Stop mixer and add flour. Mix just until combined.

3. Shape dough into logs, using about 1 1/2 teaspoons dough for each cookie. If dough is too soft to handle easily, it can be refrigerated until firm. Arrange cookies on baking sheets, leaving about 1 inch between each one. Bake until cookies are set, 12 to 14 minutes. They should be pale gold on the bottom, with little or no color on top. Cool on baking sheet for 1 minute, then transfer to a wire rack to cool completely.

4. Melt chocolate with remaining 1 tablespoon butter in a microwave oven or in top of a double boiler. Holding cookie across center, dip both ends in chocolate then in chopped nuts. Place on waxed paper until chocolate sets. Store in airtight container at cool room temperature or in refrigerator.

"How They Crumble," by Charlotte Balcomb Lane, from the *Chicago Tribune*

A molecule is the smallest particle of a substance that still has all the properties of that substance. This particle is too small to see. Can you imagine anything smaller than a molecule? Read to learn what is smaller and what makes one molecule different from another.

A water molecule is made of three atoms, as the model above represents. Two atoms are hydrogen, and one is oxygen.

Smaller than Molecules

Molecules are not all alike. There are many different kinds. A molecule of water is not the same as a molecule of wood or oil or sugar. Molecules are made up of different kinds of very tiny things called *atoms*.

Atoms are even smaller than molecules. Here is a way to get an idea how small atoms really are. Pretend you are flying in a plane high, high in the sky. Look down. It seems as though you are flying over a big, green carpet. The carpet looks flat and smooth.

Now your plane starts coming down toward the earth. Soon the green carpet begins to look different. It is no longer as smooth as it seemed when you were high up. It seems to be all bumps and holes. As you come closer and closer, you can see that the bumps are trees. Just before your plane lands, you get an even closer look at them. Then you see that they have thousands of small leaves.

When you were far away, the forest looked like a flat green carpet. As soon as you could get near it, you could see that the carpet was really made up of trees with many little leaves. The leaves were always moving and waving and wiggling. But from high up, you could not see them at all.

This story of the forest helps you to understand a little about molecules. The trees in the forest were too small for you to see from far away. Molecules are too small for you to see at all. But just as you know that trees have leaves, you can believe that molecules are made up of atoms.

A molecule is just a group of atoms that stick together. Some molecules are made up of only two atoms. Other molecules have many atoms in them. There are some kinds of molecules that have thousands of atoms in each one. A molecule of water has just three atoms in it. A molecule of sugar has 45 atoms in it. A molecule of egg white has 653 atoms in it.

Molecules are put together out of atoms the way words are put together out of letters of the alphabet. The words you use every day are made of letters that are joined in different ways. There is a different set of letters for each word. There are only 26 letters in the alphabet, but they can be used to make up many thousands of words.

That is the way atoms are joined to make many kinds of materials. There are only about *100 kinds* of atoms. But that is enough. It is enough to make a different set of atoms for every single kind of material around you. For instance, there is a certain set of atoms in a molecule of chalk. There is one set for water and another set for sugar.

Chemists work with atoms. They know how to take atoms from some molecules and put them into others. They make new molecules. That is how they discover materials that were never known before. That is how they make new plastics, new medicines, and many other new things. Chemists were able to make special metals for rocket engines when they put together certain kinds of atoms in a new way.

Different materials in the world are made up of different kinds of molecules. And each kind of molecule has its own special set of atoms stuck together in their own special way.

From *The Story of the Atom*, by Mae and Ira Freeman

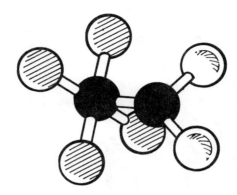

In this model representing a vinegar molecule, notice how many there are of each different type of atom. The black spheres stand for carbon atoms.

What Is Vinegar?

The smallest quantity of vinegar that can exist and still have the chemical and physical properties of vinegar is called a *molecule*. A molecule is then the smallest amount of any matter that can be identified by chemical and physical properties as that particular kind of matter and no other kind.

Vinegar needs the combined services of three substances in order to be what it is. It needs carbon, hydrogen, and oxygen in order to have the chemical and physical properties that make vinegar, vinegar. These necessary substances are called *elements*. Elements are the substances from which all matter is made.

Now, vinegar needs these three elements in a definite combination if it is going to act like vinegar. A definite amount of each element goes into each molecule of vinegar. It needs so many bits or pieces of carbon, hydrogen, and oxygen. These pieces or amounts are called *atoms*. Atoms are the smallest particle of an element.

This diagram tries to picture the chemical breakdown of vinegar. You can see that eight atoms of three different elements come together to make a molecule of vinegar. This method of seeing the pieces helps chemists develop chemical descriptions or formulas. The chemical formula for vinegar is $C_2H_4O_2$. This means two atoms of carbon, four atoms of hydrogen, and two atoms of oxygen.

This is an example of how atoms do the job of making things what they are. It helps you find the answer to "What is vinegar?"

From *Exploring and Understanding Chemistry,* by Charles D. Neal, James N. Cummins, and Charles R. Heinz

Water

Have you seen or heard water referred to as H_2O? What do you think it means? Read this selection to find out about H_2O, the most common substance on earth.

Water is everywhere. It covers almost three-fourths of the earth's surface. And even more water is found in the ice caps around the North and South poles, in the clouds above the earth, and in huge underground pools called aquifers. Water is the only substance on earth that is found naturally in three states—as a liquid, as a solid (in the form of ice), and as a gas (in the form of water vapor).

Water is the most common substance on earth—and the most important. All living things depend on water. Water also helps create our weather, and flowing water changes the face of the earth. For people, water helps grow crops, drives machinery, and provides transportation and recreation.

But the earth's water supply is not evenly distributed. In some places, people's demand for water exceeds the supply. People have also polluted (dirtied) their water supplies and made them unfit to use. Today people have begun to work toward solving these water problems.

What Water Is and How It Acts

A single drop of water is made up of millions of tiny bits called molecules. A water molecule is so tiny that you cannot see it, even with a powerful microscope.

And each water molecule is made up of even smaller bits called atoms. The largest part of a water molecule is an atom of the element oxygen. Attached to this large atom are two small atoms of hydrogen.

Chemists use letters to represent each kind of atom in a molecule, and they use numbers to show how many of these atoms are in the molecule. The symbol chemists use for water is H_2O. The letter *H* is the symbol for hydrogen, and the number *2* tells you that there are two hydrogen atoms. The letter *O* stands for oxygen.

What holds the atoms together? Atoms of hydrogen and atoms of oxygen are attracted to each other by a tendency to share parts of each other. One oxygen atom and two hydrogen atoms share parts of each other as they form a molecule of water. Bound together in this way, the hydrogen atoms take on a slightly positive electrical charge. The oxygen atom takes on a slightly negative electrical charge.

Further, the positive end of the molecule (where the hydrogen atoms are) is slightly attracted to the negative end of another water molecule (where the oxygen atom is). This force of attraction, which is called a *hydrogen bond,* causes the molecules to cluster. Snowflakes, which are frozen water, form as six-pointed stars because the hydrogen bond forces molecules of water to bind together in that shape.

The Forms of Water

Hydrogen and oxygen are both gases. Yet when two atoms of hydrogen and an atom of oxygen combine, they form a liquid—water. But water does not always remain in a liquid state. At temperatures above 100° C (212° F), it becomes a gas. At temperatures below 0° C (32° F), it is ice, a solid.

How does water change from one form to another? The molecules of water are always in motion. They vibrate and move about constantly. Near the surface of the water, some molecules break away from the pack and fly out into the air as water vapor. This change from liquid to gas is called *evaporation*. As the molecules escape, less liquid water is left. In time, all the water may evaporate.

Some water vapor is always found in air. The warmer the air, the more water vapor it can hold. You can capture some water vapor this way: Fill a dry glass with ice cubes, and wait a few minutes. Drops of water will form on the outside of the glass. They have formed there because the coldness of the glass cooled the air nearby and caused the water vapor in it to change back into a liquid. This change from gas to liquid is called *condensation*.

The higher the temperature of the water, the faster the molecules vibrate, and the faster water evaporates. When water reaches its boiling point—a temperature of 100° C (212° F)—the molecules vibrate so rapidly that they shoot apart with great force, creating hot water vapor, called steam.

Water vapor is an invisible gas. The white cloud just beyond the spout of a kettle is often incorrectly called steam. This cloud is formed of tiny droplets of water that condensed as the water vapor was cooled by the surrounding air. In the same way, you may see your breath form a pale cloud on a cold day. Your warm breath contains water vapor. The cold air causes the water vapor to condense into a cloud of tiny water droplets.

Dew, the water that forms on plants and grass on summer nights, is another example of condensation. During the day, the ground and the air are warmed by the sun. The air is able to hold considerable water vapor. At night the ground cools faster than the air, and the ground cools the air near it. The excess water vapor in this cooled air condenses on the ground, forming dew.

As water is cooled, its molecules vibrate more slowly. When the water is cooled to 0° C (32° F), the molecules stay in one place. The water freezes and becomes ice. If you could see the molecules in a block of ice, you would see the hydrogen bonds holding the molecules in a rigid, three-dimensional[1] pattern as shown in the diagram at the top of the next page.

Water contracts as it gets colder. Most liquids do the same. But below 4° C (39° F), water begins to expand again. When the water freezes, it expands by a large amount—enough to burst metal water pipes.

---

1. **three-dimensional:** having depth, height, and width

In the solid form of ice, water molecules stay in a regular pattern. In their liquid state, water molecules move freely past one another. In the form of gas, or water vapor, the molecules move about quickly and in all directions.

Water is the only common substance that expands, and therefore becomes lighter, when it freezes. This uncommon quality of water is very important to life. When a lake or river freezes, the ice forms at the surface of the water. Because it is lighter than the liquid water, it floats. The ice layer insulates[2] the water below, preventing it from freezing. This protects the fish and other living things in the water below.

The Importance of Water

Water is so common that in many parts of the world, people take its presence for granted. Yet without ample water, our lives would be very different. Indeed, life itself could not exist without water.

Water and Living Things

Scientists think that life began in water—in the prehistoric oceans. It is certain that all living things need water. Watery solutions carry nutrients throughout individual plants and animals. The nutrients are turned, through chemical processes, into energy, or they are used to build new tissues. Then the watery solutions

2. **Insulates:** prevents transfer of heat; in this case, keeps from losing heat

carry away the waste products of the chemical processes.

Water is the most important substance in the human body. It makes up about 70 percent of your body weight. If you weigh 36 kilograms (80 pounds), the water in your body accounts for 25 kilograms (about 55 pounds). Your blood is almost all water. And large parts of your skin, bones, and other body tissues are water, too.

If the amount of water in your body is reduced by just one or two percent, you feel very thirsty. With a five percent loss, your skin would shrink, you would find it hard to move your muscles, and you could not think clearly. A person would die if the amount of water fell by more than 10 percent. People can survive only a few days without water.

To stay healthy, each person needs to take in at least 2 liters (more than 2 quarts) of water every day. About half this amount comes from the water and other liquids you drink. Milk, for example, is 87 percent water. Solid foods provide about a third of the water needed by the body. For example, bread is 30 percent water, steak is 60 percent water, potatoes are 90 percent water, and tomatoes are 95 percent water. The rest of the water needed each day is produced by the body itself. As the cells of your body use food to produce energy, they produce a certain amount of water.

The body also needs to get rid of waste water. Most of the waste water—almost 2 liters—is excreted as urine. Some water also leaves the body as water vapor when you breathe and as sweat when you perspire.

All animals take in and excrete water. But some have unusual water requirements. The kangaroo rat, for example, is a desert animal that never drinks water. Its diet consists of dry seeds and other foods that contain little water. It meets its water needs as it burns food for energy. Its only sweat glands are on the pads of its toes, so it loses almost no water through perspiration.

A camel can go an entire winter without drinking any water. It produces most of the water it requires in its own body. When a camel needs water but none is available, its body begins to burn the fat in its hump. This produces enough water to keep the camel alive until it can drink.

All plants also need water. Most plants have thin hairs that extend out from their roots. Water from the soil passes through these root hairs and enters the plant's water transport system. Some of the water that is used in the plant's chemical processes is released through tiny openings in the leaves, called *stomata*. An amazing amount of water is released in this way. A single oak tree can release as much as 600 liters (almost 160 gallons) of water daily.

"Water," by Melvin Burger, from *The New Book of Knowledge*

Water Trivia

1. Of all the earth's water, how much is in oceans or seas?
2. How much of the world's water is frozen and therefore unusable?
3. Does water regulate the earth's temperature?
4. How much of the earth's water is suitable for drinking water?
5. Is it possible for me to drink water that was part of the dinosaur era?
6. How long can a person live without food and how long can a person live without water?
7. How much water is used to flush a toilet?
8. How much water is used in the average five-minute shower?
9. How much water is used to brush your teeth?
10. How much water is used on the average for an automatic dishwasher?
11. On the average, how much water is used to hand wash dishes?
12. How much water does the average home use during a year?
13. How much water does a person use daily?
14. How much water does it take to process a quarter pound of hamburger?
15. How much water does it take to process one chicken?
16. How much water does it take to process one can of fruit or vegetables?
17. What is the total amount of water used to manufacture a new car, including tires?
18. How much water does it take to make one pound of plastic?
19. How much water does it take to make one pound of wool or cotton?
20. How much water does it take to refine one barrel of crude oil?

1. 97 percent	11. 20 gallons
2. 2 percent	12. 107,000 gallons
3. Yes, it is a natural insulator.	13. 123 gallons
4. 1 percent	14. Approximately 1 gallon
5. Yes	15. 11.6 gallons
6. More than a month without food; approximately one week without water, depending on conditions	16. 9.3 gallons
7. 2–7 gallons	17. 39,090 gallons
8. 25–50 gallons	18. 24 gallons
9. 2 gallons	19. 101 gallons
10. 9–12 gallons	20. 1,851 gallons

From a fact sheet prepared for National Drinking Water Week, 1990, by the American Water Works Association

What would people's lives be like without frozen foods? Not too long ago, there were no frozen foods in stores. The development of the frozen-food industry grew from the discoveries of a clever and persistent man. Read about the unusual way he got the idea for frozen foods.

Frozen Foods

In the days before World War II, American supermarkets boasted very few quick-frozen foods. Strawberries were available only in June; green beans and other vegetables could be bought only in season. Few people outside of Louisiana had ever heard of okra. You had to go to your fish market to buy lobster and other seafood, and orange juice was squeezed each morning from fresh oranges.

But during the 1940s and 1950s a quiet but important "revolution" took place in America's eating habits and in the country's food industry too. The revolution began when quick-frozen foods were first introduced. The American housewife tried them and liked them. Today, as a result, everyone expects every type of fish, fruit, and vegetable to be available at any time of year, not only at home, but in school cafeterias and in fine restaurants.

The man responsible for this revolution was an explorer, an inventor, and a businessman. He was born in Brooklyn and he grew up in Gloucester, Massachusetts. His name was Clarence "Bob" Birdseye. As two words—"Birds Eye"—it is printed on hundreds of packages in the frozen-food compartments of supermarkets.

Bob Birdseye records data on an experiment.

When Bob Birdseye was 26, he joined with the noted Arctic missionary-physician Sir Wilfred Grenfell on a fur-trading expedition to the frozen wastes of Labrador, the windswept highlands that form the northeastern stretches of Canada. Bob was married by this time, and he and his wife and infant son settled down in a small home in the wilderness of this cheerless northland. Bob trapped furs and traded them. He owned a schooner[1] and sailed as a fisherman. In addition, he conducted a fish and wildlife survey for the United States Government.

Life in Labrador was rugged for the young Birdseye family. Fish, which thrived in great numbers in the coastal waters, was the mainstay of the Birdseye family diet. There was some meat—mostly caribou, a type of reindeer. Fresh vegetables were a rare treat and available only when a supply ship brought them in.

But it was not too long before Bob learned how to make his treasured vegetables last as long as possible. When the supply ship arrived, he would purchase such foods as cabbage by the barrelful. He stood the barrel near the back door of his home and filled it with salt water. In the subzero temperatures, the cabbages and salt water quickly hardened into a solid mass. Throughout the long, bleak Labradorian winter, whenever the family menu called for cabbage, Bob would go outside to the frozen barrel, and with a hatchet would chop a cabbagehead out. To the delight

---

1. schooner: sailing ship with two masts

of the Birdseye family, they found that the cabbage remained fresh and flavorful.

Bob also found that when he was fishing through the ice in temperatures far below zero, the fish would freeze solid before he could get them off the hook. And when he thawed the fish two or three months later, he and his family found them to be as fresh and as delicately flavored as the day they were caught. Bob knew he had stumbled on an important discovery.

Bob learned to freeze many types of vegetables and meats, and soon the Birdseye table could boast a wide variety of foods. He was excited about his experiments, and so he returned to the United States to continue his studies and to attempt to sell frozen-food products to the American public.

The basic principle of food-freezing had been known since the earliest times. But what Bob Birdseye discovered with his frozen barrel of cabbage was the secret of *quick-freezing*. He found that quick-freezing halted the tendency that all foods have to go bad. Moreover, it destroyed none of the goodness of the food. Almost any food product that could be quick-frozen remained tender and filled with its original high flavor.

Bob Birdseye's early efforts at profiting from his discovery were not very successful. It took him several years to perfect a quick-freezing process that could duplicate the conditions that nature provided in frozen Labrador. But by 1923, Bob was ready to go into business, and he set up shop in New York City to freeze and sell fresh fish, a product that he knew a great deal about. However, the public showed little desire to buy fish in frozen form. Bob's first venture in the food business ended in failure.

A man ice fishing

Bettmann Archives

But Bob was convinced he was on the right track. He moved his operations to Gloucester, Massachusetts, and always a persuasive man, he was able to get

The frozen-food section in a modern supermarket is proof of how much the industry began by Bob Birdseye has grown.

financial backing for his ideas. This time his efforts were successful; his company froze, packed, and sold fresh fish by the ton.

In 1929, Bob sold his manufacturing plant, his warehouse, and the rights to all his ideas to the General Foods Corporation. He received more than a million dollars as his share, and he was named to head the General Foods Laboratory in Gloucester.

One spring day in the following year, 1930, General Foods introduced 26 different kinds of frozen-food products in 10 grocery stores in Springfield, Massachusetts. Most of the foods were meats and seafoods, but also included were peas, strawberries, and spinach. The revolution in the food industry in America had begun.

The frozen-food industry grew steadily through the 1930s—but it grew slowly. It was not until World War II that frozen foods became popular. What happened was that hundreds of American women who went to work to support the war effort no longer had time to shop leisurely or to spend long hours preparing meals. They turned to frozen foods. Quickly they came to appreciate the fact that they were so easy to prepare.

Many other Americans first came to know of frozen foods while serving in the armed forces during World War II. About 40 percent of frozen foods packaged during 1943 and 1944 was bought by the government for the army, navy, and Marine Corps. By the end of the war, there were few American families who did not know and like frozen foods. After the war, sales boomed.

Today frozen foods are a mainstay of the American diet. Not only vegetables and fruits and fish, but poultry, meats, food and soup concentrates, and a wide variety of precooked frozen dishes are available at your food store. New and unusual types of frozen foods appear in growing numbers with every passing month.

Bob Birdseye always said that the credit for discovering the principle of quick-frozen foods should have gone to the Eskimos. They used the idea for centuries, Bob claimed, before the process was passed on to him. Bob Birdseye died in 1956. When he died, the frozen-food industry was more than a billion-dollar-a-year business. He lived long enough to see his plans and even many of his dreams become exciting realities.

From *How Do They Make It?* by George Sullivan

Unit 4: Earth Science

*the science that deals with the study of the earth
or one or more of its parts*

PLAIN OF AUVERS, Vincent vanGogh, 1890, Carnegie Museum of Art.
Acquired through the generosity of the Sarah Mellon Scaife family, 68.18

Comstock

The Earth
We Live On

If you could make a journey to the center of the earth, what do you think you would find along the way? Read to discover the picture scientists have formed of the inside of our planet.

Inside Our Planet

One way of finding out what lies beneath our feet is to dig downward. Boreholes and mine shafts have allowed us to see what the earth is like down to a depth of about eight kilometers (five miles). Down to that depth the earth is made of rock. Rock is usually a very hard, rigid substance, which makes it difficult to believe that the earth is always on the move.

Rock is made up of crystals[1] of various minerals.[2] Some rocks are made up of pieces of other rocks. These are the sedimentary rocks, and they are formed from the particles of rock worn away by erosion.[3] These particles were carried down toward seas, lakes, or low-lying areas, where they gradually piled up, and over many years became squeezed into layers of solid rock. Other kinds of rock

---

1. **crystals:** particles of solid material whose atoms are arranged in a regular repeating pattern
2. **minerals:** natural substances, such as coal and ore, that are not plants, animals, or other living things
3. **erosion:** a slow eating or wearing away by moving water or wind

The Mount Saint Helens volcano erupting in Washington state in 1980

appear to have crystallized from what was once molten, or liquid, material.

Rock is not entirely rigid, though. An engineer would say that it has "elastic properties." That is not to say that rock is like a rubber ball, but it will bend, very slightly. And although it is strong, rock is likely to break if given a sudden, sharp shock.

So, the earth appears to have a rigid, rather brittle *crust*. Is it like that all the way down? Because no one has ever actually been to the center of the earth to see what it is like, scientists have had to do a lot of detective work to find out.

First of all there is the difference in temperature and pressure. Early miners found that as they went down into mine shafts, it got hotter. This was one clue that led scientists to believe temperatures toward the center of the earth could be very high. The clearest signal, though, came from erupting volcanoes that threw up fiery, liquid rock. As the molten rock cooled, it became hard and formed igneous rock. Finding igneous rock on

Comstock

the earth's surface gave another clue to the scientists of the conditions deep inside.

The sheer weight of rock inside the earth means that pressure, too, is very high. This gets higher toward the center.

Nowadays, scientists do not believe that the earth is as hot as they once thought. But the center of the earth is still pretty warm! The latest estimate is that temperatures in the center are about 4,300° C (7,800° F).

The Earth's Weight

In the nineteenth century, a man called J. H. Poynting invented a very ingenious[4] balance that he used to weigh the earth. He worked out its weight to be many millions of tons, and also proved that whatever the earth is made of deep down is very heavy indeed. Scientists believe that the earth's *core* is probably made up of iron and nickel.

Over the years, scientists have built

---

4. Ingenious: clever

up a picture of the earth's interior. The hard, rigid outer part that we live on is the crust. This is from about 10 kilometers (six miles) to 40 kilometers (25 miles) deep under the oceans, and about 70 kilometers (44 miles) deep under the continents or land masses. The continental crust stands up high, and has "roots" reaching deep down into the earth. Below the crust is a layer called the *mantle*. This is made up mainly of igneous rock, and it reaches down 2,900 kilometers (1,800 miles) to the core. The core itself is divided into two parts; the outer part is liquid, and the inner part is solid.

As far as movement is concerned, the part of the earth that is most important is the upper part of the mantle. The crust is rigid, but the upper part of the mantle is not. Scientists think that perhaps as much as 10 percent of this region may be liquid rock. It is certainly the source of the molten rock that comes pouring out of volcanoes as lava and cools to form masses of solidified igneous rock such as granite.

This zone, which reaches down to about 250 kilometers (155 miles), is called the *upper mantle*. No one is sure what it is actually like. It could be a sort of slush of solid crystals with liquid rock around them, or it might be like soft modeling clay. But whatever it is like in detail, it has one very important property: it can move. Very, very slowly, great currents are at work in the upper mantle, gradually moving material around as they carry heat from deep within the earth up toward the surface.

From *Mountains and Earth Movements,* by Iain Bain

Can you name the six continents? The title of this selection may provide a clue to what scientists believe is happening to the continents. Read to learn how the six continents—North America, South America, Eurasia (Europe and Asia labeled as one), Africa, Australia, and Antarctica—may have come to be where they are today.

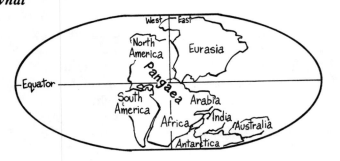

200 million years ago

Moving

Here is a game that you can play. Find an atlas with a map of the world. Trace the outlines of the continents and cut them out of your tracing paper. Now push the continents together and see if you can make them fit into one great island landmass. In some places the continents will fit together with difficulty, but in others, like South America and Africa, the fit will be surprisingly good.

What you have done on paper is what people have been doing in their imaginations ever since they had maps that accurately showed the proper shape of the continents. However, today it is more than a game. Scientists really do believe that the continents have moved.

The possibility that South America and Africa were once joined has been discussed for centuries. Toward the end of the last century, a geologist named Edward Suess suggested that once there had been a great southern continent, which he called Gondwanaland. This had broken up, he said, and the various parts had drifted away from each other to form the landmasses we know today.

The idea of *continental drift* was taken further early this century, when a German scientist, called Alfred Wegener, showed that rocks and fossils in Africa and South America were very similar. He said that this was a sign that the two continents had once been joined. Very few people took him seriously, even

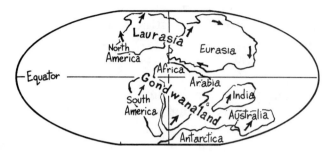

135 million years ago

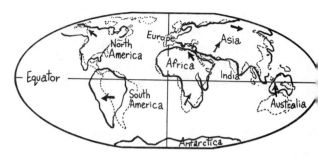

The broken outlines above show the positions of the continents today. The solid outlines show where the continents may be 50 million years from now.

Continents

though geologists and explorers were by then finding proof that the continents had once been closer together.

The problem was that nobody, not even Wegener, could work out how or why the continents moved. Today we know that the upper mantle below the crust is capable of moving, but in those days they believed it was quite rigid. If it was rigid how could the continents move? Also, Wegener believed that it was only the continental crust areas that moved. His idea was that the continents "drifted" through the oceanic crust. Since everyone believed that the crust beneath the oceans was also rigid, this made Wegener's theory very difficult to accept.

One Super-Continent

Yet the evidence piled up to show that at one time the earth's continents had been joined. Wegener's idea (like that of Edward Suess before him) was that about 200 million years ago, all the world's continents had been joined together in one super-continent, which he named Pangaea. Scientists studying the development, or evolution, of plants and animals discovered that many of them had evolved in the same way, up to the time when Wegener believed Pangaea had broken up. After that time they had started to evolve differently. There were also signs that, millions of years ago, parts of the world had climates very different from those they have now. The polar regions once had tropical climates, and in what are now hot places, such as Africa, India, and Australia, there was snow and ice.

Soon after came the idea that currents flowed in the upper mantle, and that it was not entirely rigid after all. At last Wegener's ideas were accepted, although not until long after his death.

The final proof that the continents moved came from under the sea. Scientists had known for years that there were great underwater mountain ranges in the middle of the world's oceans. In these *mid-ocean ridges* were active volcanoes, and scientists believed this was where material in the upper mantle burst through to form new crust.

When scientists dated the rocks that formed the seabed, they found that as they moved farther away from each side of the ridges the rocks got older. So it seemed that new crust was being formed on the ridges, and that new sea floor was spreading outward.

The idea of continental drift had now turned into the idea of *tectonic[1] plate movement*. Today, scientists believe that the earth's crust is divided up into about 12 tectonic plates, which include both oceanic crust and continental crust. Some of the plates are very large. For instance, Europe and Asia are part of one plate.

The plates are all moving slowly. They are mostly pulling apart at the mid-ocean ridges; in other places they are sliding past each other, and in some areas they are actually colliding.

The speeds at which they move have been calculated. The North Atlantic, for instance, is spreading at about two centimeters (one inch) per year. India is crashing into Asia at more than five centimeters (two inches) per year, in places. The fastest movement is in the southeast Pacific, where the Pacific plate and the Nazca plate are moving apart at more than 18 centimeters (seven inches) per year.

---

1. **tectonic:** having to do with the forces and results of movement and change in the earth's crust

---

From *Mountains and Earth Movements*, by Iain Bain

What animal do you think is described here: a large animal with a shaggy mane, a large head with short horns, heavy front legs, and a large fleshy hump? The remains of just such an animal were found in Alaska in 1979. Read to find out about this unusual discovery of an unusual bison.

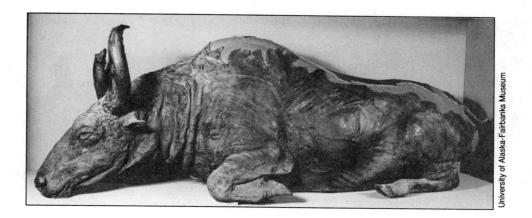

University of Alaska-Fairbanks Museum

Blue Babe—

a Messenger from the Ice Age

Uncovered during a mining operation, the carcass of an Alaska steppe bison has revealed the story of the animal's Ice Age[1] death to scientists at the University of Alaska Museum on the University of Alaska—Fairbanks (UAF) campus.

Gold miners Walter and Ruth Roman and their sons discovered the carcass in 1979 near Fairbanks, Alaska. Part of the bison was exposed as water from a hydraulic mining hose melted the frozen muck in which it was embedded. The miners, realizing the potential significance of their find, contacted the university.

Paleontologist[2] Dale Guthrie determined the carcass was of an Ice Age bison (*Bison priscus*), probably tens of thousands of years old. He decided to excavate[3] immediately in order to remove the frozen relic before it could deteriorate.

It soon became obvious that the bison carcass could not be excavated quickly because of frozen ground and the close proximity of large ice wedges.

---

1. **Ice Age:** period of time 10,000 to 1.8 million years ago, during which ice eroded the land, many large mammals became extinct, and human beings appeared
2. **paleontologist:** scientist who studies fossils and ancient life forms
3. **excavate:** dig out; uncover by digging

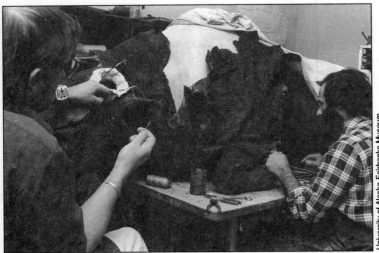

Taxidermists sew the bison's skin over a mold. Preserved this way, the animal can be put on display.

University of Alaska-Fairbanks Museum

The bison carcass was covered with a blue chalky substance when it was discovered and excavated. A mineral coating of white vivianite was produced when phosphorus from the animal tissue reacted with iron in the soil surrounding the bison. When the vivianite was exposed to air, it turned to a brilliant blue, earning the bison the nickname Blue Babe, after Paul Bunyan's[4] giant blue ox.

A radiocarbon date[5] from a piece of skin shows that the bison died 36,000 years ago. Claw marks on the rear of the carcass and tooth punctures in the skin indicate that the bison was killed by an Ice Age American lion (*Panthera leo atrox*), an ancestor of the living African lion.

The lion opened the bison from the side, peeling back the skin and exposing the vertebrae, ribs, and upper limbs. The muscles of these areas were eaten away, allowing the bones to be pulled loose and partially scavenged by a variety of other carnivores[6] and birds such as wolves, foxes, wolverines, and ravens.

The bison appears to have died during the fall or winter when conditions were relatively cold. This was revealed

Although high summer temperatures melted several inches of soil per day, the bison remained frozen in the vertical bank for some time.

Eventually the carcass hung freely from the bank by the head and neck which were still embedded in frozen soil. Fearing the thawed portion of the bison would begin to decompose, Guthrie severed it from the head and neck, transported it to UAF and refroze it. Excavation of the head and neck continued until they also came free from the muck bank. They then were stored with the rest of the carcass.

As the frozen soils surrounding the bison melted, they were collected and screen-washed to expose bone fragments, hair, insects, wood, and plant parts. The surrounding geology, the orientation and position of the bison carcass, and all material found in association with it were recorded. The information helped in piecing together the bison's story.

---

4. **Paul Bunyan:** the lumberjack known in American tall tales for his size, his strength, and his pet, Babe the Blue Ox
5. **radiocarbon date:** a date found by measuring the amount of radioactive carbon remaining in a substance—the less that is found, the older the substance is.
6. **carnivores:** meat-eaters

from remnants of underfur and a layer of fat on the bison carcass, which provided insulation and energy during cold winter months. After the bison died, the carcass probably cooled rapidly due to cold winter temperatures and soon froze. The frozen carcass would have been extremely difficult for scavengers to eat, so it probably remained in its partially scavenged state throughout the entire winter.

The bison either died on a valley bottom or was transported there by movement of soils down slope during spring melt. Once the carcass was in a stable position on the valley bottom, it was buried by soils eroding from the surrounding hills. During the summer, small silt[7] washes probably continued to cover it.

Although the carcass was covered by seasonally warm soils, the underlying cool soil inhibited decomposition. During the following winter, the bison was encased in frozen soils. Through time, the carcass became more deeply buried and eventually part of the permafrost[8] zone. A vegetative layer developed on the surface, insulating the bison carcass from future thaw.

The preservation of this bison carcass was so exceptional coagulated pockets of blood were discovered in the skin at the base of the claw and canine teeth puncture wounds inflicted by the lion. Muscle tissue not scavenged by carnivores had a "beef jerky" texture and color. White greasy bone marrow remained in most of the long bones. The skin retained a layer of fat, although most of its hair was gone from slight decomposition. The hooves on all four feet were attached to the carcass, keeping their shape through the millennia.[9] The horn sheaths adhered firmly to the skull and were also in excellent condition.

Ice Age mammal carcasses are quite rare, but a few have been found in permafrost in Siberia and Alaska. The cold soils of the Arctic are one of nature's most effective ways of preserving animal tissue for tens of thousands of years.

Only two discoveries in permafrost, other than Blue Babe, have been reconstructed by a taxidermist[10] and put on display in the world. These are a juvenile woolly mammoth and an adult woolly mammoth, both in the Zoological Museum in Leningrad. Blue Babe can be seen at the UA Museum. The head and forequarters of a baby woolly mammoth were recovered in Fairbanks in the 1950s and are now in a refrigerated display at the American Museum of Natural History in New York.

---

7. **silt:** loose, tiny particles carried along by moving water
8. **permafrost:** a layer of permanently frozen subsoil found in most of the arctic regions
9. **millennia:** periods of thousands of years
10. **taxidermist:** an expert in preparing the skins of dead animals, stuffing and mounting them so that they look alive

---

"Blue Babe," by Gary Selinger, from the *University of Alaska Magazine*

You've probably heard and talked about the climate in your area many times. However, have you ever really thought about what climate is? Read the following selection to learn about the factors that affect climate.

What Makes Climates Change?

Most people know that climate has to do with the weather. So, in order to understand climate, you have to know something about weather.

WEATHER

All weather takes place in the atmosphere—the blanket of air that surrounds the earth. Weather can be defined as the condition of the atmosphere at a particular time and place. Weather is produced by a combination of different factors, such as temperature, air pressure,[1] wind, and moisture. Perhaps the most important of these factors are temperature and moisture.

---

1. air pressure: force caused by the weight of the atmosphere

Temperature

The earth receives its heat from the sun. The sun's rays heat the earth's surface, and the air is then heated by the warm ground or water beneath it. However, the earth's surface is not heated evenly. There are two main reasons for this uneven heating: (1) the angle at which the sun's rays hit the surface and (2) the type of material the rays hit. Take a closer look now at these two factors.

Angle of the Sun's Rays. If the earth's surface were flat, the sun's rays would hit the surface at the same angle everywhere. However, the earth is a sphere; its surface is curved. This curved shape causes the sun's rays to hit different parts of the surface at different angles. Because the sun is almost directly over the equator, the sun's rays hit the surface near the equator straight on, at almost no slant. As you travel away from the equator, the curve of the earth's surface causes the sun's rays to hit the surface at more of a slant. The polar regions receive the most slanted rays of the sun.

Direct rays heat the earth's surface better than slanted rays do. Although all of the sun's rays carry the same amount of energy, the energy carried by slanted rays is spread out over a larger area than the energy carried by direct rays. You can demonstrate this idea by shining a flashlight onto a sheet of paper. From a distance of about eight inches

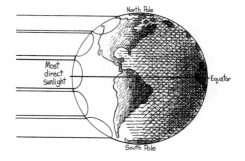

The sun's rays striking the earth

(about 20 centimeters), shine the light directly onto the paper. Check the size, shape, and brightness of the lighted area of the paper. Trace the lighted area with a pencil. Now without moving the light, tilt the paper away from the light at an angle of about 45°. What happens to the size, shape, and brightness of the lighted area of the paper?

In both cases, you have the same amount of light hitting the paper. Now imagine that the light is changed to heat. The same amount of heat would be produced in both cases. However, on the slanted paper, the heat would be spread out over a larger area. The temperature of that lighted area would be lower than the temperature of the brightly lighted circle.

In much the same way, the rays that strike the earth's surface near the equator do the best job of heating, while the rays that hit the surface at a slant near the poles do the poorest job. This helps explain why places near the equator are so warm and places near the poles are so cold.

Type of Material. Some materials heat up and cool down faster than other materials. Have you ever put your hand on a car that has been sitting in the sun? You know that the car feels very hot—hotter, for example, than a wooden bench sitting right beside the car.

The earth's surface consists of many different materials, both natural and manufactured. For our purposes, however, we need only consider two materials, land (soil and rocks) and water. The sun's rays heat both the land and the water. However, land heats up faster than water. It also cools faster than water. This fact contributes to the uneven heating of the earth's surface. In spring and summer, land heats up much faster than water, and it reaches much higher temperatures. In fall and winter, the land cools faster than the water, and it reaches much lower temperatures.

The effect of the uneven heating of the earth's surface is to set air in motion. Moving air is called wind. In places where the earth's surface is warm, air above that surface is heated and expands. This causes the air to become lighter, or less dense, than the air around it. Cooler, heavier air moves in along the surface and takes the place of the warm air, forcing the warmer air to rise. In places where the earth's surface is cool, air near the surface is cooled, becomes heavier (denser) than the air around it, and sinks. When the cooled air settles to the earth's surface, it moves out along the surface as wind. As you can see, winds generally move from cooler to warmer regions of the earth's surface.

Moisture

Moisture is a term sometimes used to indicate water in all its forms. You have already learned about the importance of liquid water in contributing to the uneven heating of the earth's surface.

In the atmosphere, where weather takes place, water is found in all three of its states—liquid, solid, and gas. Clouds are made up of very tiny droplets of liquid water or crystals of ice. Fog is a cloud that forms at the earth's surface. Water falls from clouds as liquid rain or solid snow, hail, or sleet. But all of the liquid and solid water found in the atmosphere is formed from water vapor.

Water vapor is the name given to water in the gaseous state. When liquid water is warmed, some of the water leaves the surface of the liquid and changes to water vapor, which is a gas. This process is called evaporation. All air—even air over the driest desert—contains some water vapor. Most of the water vapor in the air is produced by the evaporation of liquid water from oceans, lakes, and streams. So air near large bodies of water usually contains more water vapor than does air over the centers of continents.

Sometimes you can "feel" the water vapor in the air. It is water vapor that produces the uncomfortable "sticky" feeling on a hot summer day. Warm air can hold more water vapor than cool air can. Thus, when warm, moist air cools, some of the water vapor is "squeezed" out of the air and changes back to a liquid. This process is called condensation. Clouds form by condensation of water vapor in the air at high altitudes.

CLIMATE

Weather was defined earlier as the condition of the atmosphere at a particular time and place. You know from experience that the weather at any particular place changes from day to day. Climate, on the other hand, is the *average* weather conditions of an area over a long period of time.

The climate in any region is determined by two basic conditions—temperature and precipitation, or rainfall. These conditions, in turn, are influenced by several different factors.

Factors That Affect Temperature

Latitude is a measure of distance north and south of the equator. As you have learned, regions near the equator receive the most direct rays of the sun. These regions have a warm climate. Regions near the poles receive the most slanted rays of the sun, and thus they have the lowest average temperature and the coolest climates.

Altitude is height, or distance, above sea level. Because the air is heated by the earth's surface, temperatures become cooler as distance from the surface increases. This fact explains why some high mountain peaks remain covered with snow all year, even in regions near the equator.

Large bodies of water affect the temperature of nearby land areas. Water heats up and cools down more slowly than land, and this has a moderating effect on the air temperatures over the nearby land. Winters tend to be milder and summers cooler in areas near the water.

Ocean currents are like swift "rivers" flowing in the ocean. Currents moving from the equator toward the poles are warm water currents. Currents moving from the poles toward the equator are cold water currents. These currents affect the temperatures of nearby land areas.

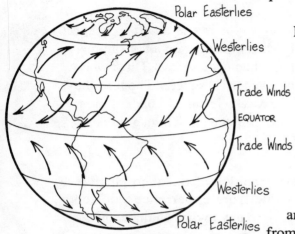

The belts of prevailing winds

Factors That Affect Precipitation

Prevailing winds are winds that blow almost constantly in the same direction. These winds, which are found in a series of belts at the earth's surface, are set in motion by the uneven heating of the surface. Winds that blow from ocean areas toward the land usually carry large amounts of moisture. Winds that blow from land areas toward the ocean usually carry little moisture.

Mountain ranges act as barriers to prevailing winds. They cause the winds to rise. If moist air is forced to rise up over a mountain range, the air will cool and much of its water vapor will condense. Clouds will form, and most of the moisture will fall as rain or snow on the side of the mountain facing the wind. When the air reaches the side of the mountain away from the wind, it will be carrying very little moisture. Thus, that side of the mountain will receive very little rainfall and will have a dry climate.

CHANGING CLIMATES

Can climates change? Could a desert someday become a tropical paradise? Could glaciers form at the equator? Given enough time, just about anything is possible. We know that much of North America was covered by a huge ice sheet as recently as 10,000 years ago. And fossils of tropical plants have been found near the South Pole. You now know about the factors that determine and influence climate. Any event or events that cause a change in any of these factors could

trigger a series of events leading to a change in climate. In the past, worldwide changes in climate may have been caused by such natural factors as the slow movement of the continents across the surface of the earth or changes in the energy released by the sun. These factors could produce climate changes in the future.

Some minor changes in climate might be caused by changes in prevailing wind patterns or ocean currents. But what about changes caused by human activities? Many scientists believe that the burning of fossil fuels, such as coal and oil, is causing a gradual increase in the temperature of the atmosphere. If true, this global warming could lead to the melting of the polar icecaps, a rise in the level of the oceans, and dramatically altered climatic conditions around the globe.

Written by Publicom, Inc./Maurice J. Sabean

Space Junk

The title of this selection
suggests what one of our newest pollution
problems is. What kinds of objects do you think people have left
in space? Read to find out why polluting
space can be dangerous.

Time: the present.

Place: a few hundred miles above Earth.

You're traveling through space. All around you is a black sky that never grows light. In the distance you see the moon, the sun, and the stars. Beneath you, Earth is softly glowing, spinning silently in a blue-green haze.

But suddenly a flash of light dazzles you. It's getting brighter and brighter—it's hurtling right toward you.

You and your fellow astronauts watch it approach, unable to move. What could it be? An alien spaceship? An enemy missile? A falling star?

The light streaks closer and closer. Now you're really getting worried. In the cabin of your spacecraft you all hold your breath. Then someone hits a button on the instrument panel, and on the screen in front of you, you suddenly see what the light is. You and the other astronauts start laughing. It's only a screwdriver, lost in space—just another

piece of space junk, like the ones you've seen before.

Funny? Yes. Science fiction fantasy? Not really. All kinds of man-made clutter are circling the planet Earth right now—we even know a screwdriver was once in orbit. And although astronauts today can't actually identify each hunk of trash the way they do in this imaginary scene, space junk is a real danger to them and to the world's space programs.

How did it all get up there? Why didn't anybody stop it?

When burned-out rocket stages kept circling Earth, or satellites stopped working but didn't fall from the sky, nobody worried too much about it. After all, people told themselves, space stretched on and on, like an empty ocean that never reaches a shore. When flecks of paint peeled off spacecraft or when astronauts on spacewalks dropped some of their tools, nobody thought it would be a problem.

But even though space seems to go on forever, we depend on the part of it that is closest to the surface of the earth.

In the same way our air and water have grown dirty over the years, this fraction of space closest to our planet is slowly filling up with junk. Today there are millions of pieces of debris above us, from bits tinier than a thumbtack to rockets as tall as a three-story house. And every piece, even a small one, can damage a spacecraft and put the lives of astronauts in danger.

More and more garbage is created every day. Sometimes old and useless spacecraft tumble back to Earth. If one landed on a city, lives could be threatened. Sometimes rocket stages that have been traveling near the surface of the earth for years will explode. Chunks of metal then spread out hundreds of miles across our sky. Sometimes one piece of space junk crashes into another. More garbage is created and ends up traveling around the earth. Sometimes bits of debris collide with spacecraft carrying people. On one space shuttle mission a window was damaged.

So far we've been lucky. No terrible space-junk accident has occurred. But some experts feel our luck may soon run out. An American space station might be launched before the end of this century—will it ram into a hunk of junk and explode into smithereens? Special weapons that are powered by nuclear energy are being built for space—will one of them smash into floating metal and rain radiation[1] on our planet? Satellites are orbiting above us—will one crash in flames to the ground, setting fires and injuring people?

How will we get rid of all this garbage? Can scientists change the world's space program so less litter gets left behind? What are experts doing to protect spacecraft from space junk? Can we even locate all the dangerous debris up in the sky? So much of it is swimming around us that astronomers fear they might mistake bits of it for distant new stars!

If we want to stay free to explore the universe, space junk is a problem we are going to have to solve. After all, there's no space sanitation team to come to the rescue. Does this mean the garbage above us will haunt Earth forever? What are we doing to stop the pollution? Can space ever be the same now that earthlings have reached it? The future of space exploration may depend on how we answer these questions.

---

1. **radiation:** particles or waves that can harm living tissue and that are sent out as a result of the decay of atoms of certain substances

---

From *Space Junk*, by Judy Donnelly and Sydelle Kramer